📖 SCHOLASTIC

Teaching Grammar With Playful Poems

Nancy Mack

New York • Toronto • London • Auckland • Sydney
Mexico City • New Delhi • Hong Kong • Buenos Aires

Teaching
Resources

Credits:

Boa Constrictor" from *Where the Sidewalk Ends* by Shel Silverstein. Copyright © 1974 by Evil Eye Music, Inc. Reprinted by permission of HarperCollins Publishers.

"Cloud and Sky" from *Soap Soup and Other Verses* by Karla Kuskin. Copyright © 1992 by Karla Kuskin. Used by permission of HarperCollins Publishers.

"Cures for a Boring School Day" by Kalli Dakos is reprinted with the permission of Simon & Schuster Books for Young Readers, an imprint of Simon & Schuster Children's Publishing Division from *Don't Read This Book, Whatever You Do!* by Kalli Dakos. Text copyright © 1993 Kalli Dakos.

"Encounter" from *Sam's Place* by Lilian Moore. Copyright © 1973 Lilian Moore. Used by permission of Marian Reiner for the author.

"I'm Talking Big" from *Making Friends With Frankenstein* by Colin McNaughton. Reprinted by permission of Candlewick Press.

"Last Night I Dreamed of Chickens" by Jack Prelutsky from *Something Big Has Been Here*. Text copyright © 1990 by Jack Prelutsky. Used by permission of HarperCollins Publishers.

"Rebound" by Nancy Mack © 2006.

"What I Found in My Desk" by Bruce Lansky from *No More Homework! No More Tests!* by Bruce Lansky. Copyright © Bruce Lansky. Reprinted with permission from Meadowbrook Press.

Cover design by Adona Jimenez
Interior design by Kelli Thompson
Interior illustrations by Mike Moran
ISBN: 0-439-57411-0

Copyright © 2005 by Nancy Mack
All rights reserved. Printed in the U.S.A.

3 4 5 6 7 8 9 10   40   11 10 09 08

Contents

Introduction

Good teaching ideas—like good teachers—grow and change over time. Innovative teachers gather new ideas from other teachers, books, journals, magazines, Web sites, conferences, workshops, and college courses, and then they promptly make these ideas their own by changing them. We turn an idea into a unique practice when we alter it to suit our specific classroom context, including our own personalities and those of our students. We also adapt every teaching idea to our particular grade level, school environment, and community conditions. Moreover, these adaptations occur continuously as we monitor our students' responses and devise the changes necessary to increase their motivation and enhance their performance.

Through this process of adapting grammar instruction to meet the needs of my students and those of my preservice teachers, I've developed a fun but purposeful way to teach grammar in the context of poetry that upper-grade students love. The selected poetry supports district reading goals, and the language patterns in the poems highlight key grammar concepts taught in grades 3–5. Follow-up guided poetry writing activities are designed to reinforce the grammar concept and provide a manageable way for students to publish and present their writing to real audiences. My hope in writing this book is that as you work with these lessons, you will find the best ways to adapt the ideas to your specific teaching needs and environment.

About This Book

The teaching strategies I describe in this book are not the only way to teach grammar; they are one way I have discovered that really works. These particular strategies were developed after years of my frustrations as a middle-school teacher with a wide range of ineffective methods such as workbook exercises, individualized learning packets, cartoon illustrations, dramatic skits, and humorous example sentences. I may have succeeded in making grammar cute, but I still needed to work on improving student performance.

I pursued this topic further in a two-volume dissertation about cultural preferences for traditional grammar instruction. I discovered that traditional teaching methods are amazingly persistent. To illustrate this point in a nontraditional teaching context, the inmate students whom I taught through a prison program asked me if I had been fired from a regular teaching position since I had asked them to write essays rather than fill out grammar worksheets. Their expectations were that "doing English" meant single-underlining subjects and double-underlining verbs, not engaging in the actual writing of essays. Yet with all my instructional experimentation and study, I still found it a challenge to teach grammar explicitly in the context of meaningful writing. The example lessons described here were refined over a long period of time as I designed discovery mini-lessons, and they will most certainly change again as I learn more about language and teaching.

The challenge of writing a volume about classroom strategies is to design a format that allows teachers to pick and choose, leaving openings for adding, subtracting, and transforming sample activities. I encourage you to try out these strategies, researching what works for you and your students and what needs further innovation. Discuss these strategies with your colleagues and don't forget to ask your students for their reactions.

An Overview of the Lessons

In each chapter, you'll find the same lesson format, which includes the following strategies:

- Read aloud a poem with a predictable line pattern and lead students in dramatic readings.
- Model the linguistic pattern by writing a class poem.
- Teach the grammar concept through a mini-lesson that names the concept and defines and analyzes its function.
- Help students prewrite ideas for a poem topic, imitate the grammar pattern from a guided writing format, and publish the poem creatively to share with others.
- Engage students in wondering about the language patterns and discovering how grammar is used in writing.
- Reinforce grammar concepts with activities that are visual, physical, or linked to a common analogy.
- Provide extension activities for advanced exploration.
- Explore topic variations and connections to literature.

Tips for Implementing the Lessons

Imitation should precede discussions about grammar.
An error that I made with this type of lesson for years was teaching grammar terms and usage rules first—before doing the writing. Teaching a concept in isolation from its use goes against the way the brain acquires language. Starting with a lecture about grammar also decreases students' engagement

and necessitates teaching the whole lesson over again when students need it for the writing task. When teaching these lessons, I purposely hold my linguistic explanations at bay until students almost beg to know what the grammar element highlighted in the model poem is. Teaching the grammar mini-lesson after you've modeled the grammar activity or even after students have written their own pattern poem is a much better course of action than beginning with a lecture.

NEVER TEACH FROM NEGATIVE EXAMPLES.

We may all be tempted to use drill sheets containing sentences that have errors to be corrected or sentences with choices of two forms, one correct and one incorrect. Be aware that these exercises are a particularly unhelpful way to introduce a concept to students because seeing an incorrect model can cause the brain to be confused and overwhelmed. (Similarly, we would not give students math problems worked incorrectly and ask them to guess the correct method from the wrong answers.) The lessons in this book ask students to imitate a grammar pattern offered in a correct and creative model— a strategy that ensures students learn the target grammar concept and perhaps even internalize other concepts such as exceptional word choice and rhyme.

ASK DISCOVERY QUESTIONS TO HELP STUDENTS THINK REFLECTIVELY ABOUT HOW THEY USE LANGUAGE.

Presenting students with models of humorous, rich language and encouraging them to wonder why language works the way it does helps them learn grammar effectively—more effectively than if they're taught the target terms out of context. One important element of the following lessons is the Metacognitive Moment prompts, which help you initiate a discussion that gets students thinking about how they learn or understand the target grammar concept and related concepts.

The best metacognitive discussions involve spontaneous questioning from both students and from you. The "wondering" thought process clarifies patterns and conventions, helping students make connections to other, more familiar concepts that in turn helps them store new information in their long-term memories. This type of open discussion can entice students to become fascinated with language and to experiment with new sentence structures. People who are fearful of making language mistakes rarely write, and when they do, they use the simplest language possible—we want our students to be daring and masterful writers.

Actively model the wondering process; during your discussions, ask questions to which you do not know the answers. Model looking up information about grammar in reference books such as a dictionary, style book, or

> **TIP**
>
> Inquiring minds need to know things, whereas minds that have their inquiring done by others need not know a thing.

thesaurus. Before I started looking things up, I never knew that the article *the* usually appears with *most* or that *eldest* was the preferred superlative form of *old*. Here are some more questions for which I have recently sought answers: *Is it possible to make a sentence with a comparative adjective without than? Do comparatives and superlatives exist in other languages? Do other languages use suffixes? Did we get all of our suffixes from Latin?*

ENCOURAGE CREATIVE LANGUAGE USE.

You'll find some students who enjoy coming up with different sentence structures and variations on patterns. Take a moment to stand in awe of their genius. Give bonus points for alliteration or rhyme or the most words per line or the best vocabulary. Students really know a pattern when they can create an innovation on the basic pattern.

USE ANALOGIES OR OTHER MNEMONIC DEVICES TO HELP STUDENTS LEARN DIFFICULT-TO-REMEMBER GRAMMAR CONCEPTS.

When learners are faced with a problem that cannot be solved intuitively, they need to use a conscious strategy designed for clarifying the task. Because the brain can only conceptualize new things in terms of the old things it already knows, you can use mnemonic devices and comparisons as a way of consciously assisting memory. People use rhymes, knuckle counting, and other gimmicks to remember the days in a month and other helpful information—devices that often make the information stick with learners for a lifetime.

Some of the best memory devices are those created by students. When you come to a difficult concept like using an irregular verb in the past tense, encourage students to create mnemonic devices: Ask students what the definition or concept they are trying to remember is like or could be compared to. You may be impressed by their answers. For example, students might compare an action verb to a play-by-play sportscast because the verb tells the action. If students have trouble coming up with a comparison that they can remember, brainstorm some examples with them keeping in mind that we tend to remember colorful, moving, exaggerated, rhythmic, sensory, and humorous comparisons best. (For more background on the brain and language learning, see Chapter 10.)

MODEL THE CONCEPT...AND THEN MODEL SOME MORE!

If you find that the majority of students do not understand the grammar concept you've introduced, back up and model the concept for the whole group again, speaking aloud your thought process and asking them for help as you demonstrate the process (for example, how to tell an adjective from an adverb). You can further reinforce this process by having students redo the process in small groups with whole-group sharing at the end.

> **TIP**
>
> Upper-grade students excel at language innovations. This may be why slang emerges during the preteen years—the experienced language user enjoys inventing new language patterns.

> **TIP**
>
> When students struggle with a concept, model first with the whole group, second with small groups, third with pairs, and fourth one-on-one.

The talk that is done in small groups helps students transfer the peer dialogue (spoken thought process) to internal thought processes. Pair discussions can work well for students who still cannot do the process alone. And finally, a few students may need individual coaching with you and experiences with materials at a more accessible level. Keeping this framework in mind when you plan can ensure that students have successful learning experiences.

WHEN THE WRITING IS WEAK, DO MORE PREWRITING.

The following lessons involve writing activities that engage students in using each grammar concept in a meaningful context. You can never do enough prewriting. Strategies like brainstorming ideas, webbing details, sharing in pairs, freewriting, creating word banks, drawing, and role-playing will improve the quality of student writing. These strategies can be done at any time during the writing process, even at the very last minute. If students seem to be disengaged or unmotivated, try a quick prewriting activity to get everyone revved up for writing.

PLAN FOR LOTS OF SHARING.

Having students share their writing with peers while the writing is in process is crucial to their developing an understanding of language conventions and building a classroom community. Language is a social phenomenon; consequently, talking about ideas, drafts, and revisions with others helps students create the mental framework that later makes it possible to consciously revise the writing on the page. (For more background on social learning and language, see Chapter 10.)

Writing that isn't shared dies on the vine. The expectation of a significant audience outside the classroom changes the communication task in ways that can make students ask for more time and help in proofreading. You can find various audiences to whom students can show off their published writing: Students from earlier grades, local senior citizens, and community members who have expertise with related topics or work in fields connected to writing can provide great reinforcement for students' efforts.

DON'T SKIP THE ART PART.

Writing assignments are too often passed down the row to the teacher without much notice or fanfare. In contrast, these lessons provide an art-based publishing opportunity for student writing that incorporates the targeted grammar concept. Artistic publishing can take writing to a higher level. Using color, texture, shapes, glitter, gel pens, fibers, stamps, pop-ups, or other special materials can ensure commitment from students and increase their sense of satisfaction upon completion of the project. I strive each term to make at least one writing project so special that it may be remembered as a lifetime literacy event.

> **TIP**
>
> Visuals can add a symbolic element that precedes writing; students have told me that they saw in their mind's eye how they wanted to publish their writing artistically before they had even begun writing.

ASSESS GRAMMAR CONCEPTS FROM STUDENTS' WRITING AND NOT FROM A STANDARDIZED TEST.

Traditional right-wrong questions about isolated sentences measure only those skills learned in the same format; such tests do not assess the ability to write well. An engaging and informative grammar assessment of the concepts taught in these lessons may be conducted in the form of a poetry performance rather than a mastery quiz. If students must pass a standardized test on usage, first make sure students understand how to use the concepts being tested in their own writing, then practice that particular test's format and discuss test-taking strategies. Remember that the larger educational goal is to teach students to choose to write for a lifetime, not just to pass a simplistic skills test created solely to gather statistics at one brief moment in time.

Challenging Assumptions About Language Learning

Language gives human beings the potential to imagine the future, create masterpieces, relate to other people, and change the world. Each language is made up of a set of complex, dynamic systems that are endlessly interesting to study. Regretfully, traditional grammar instruction overemphasizes drill work and simplistic definitions so that most students have developed an automatic "yuck response" to the mere mention of the word *grammar*.

The following cultural myths about grammar instruction reinforce antiquated practices, making it difficult for teachers to invent better teaching methodologies. However, once we've uncovered reliable information about language learning, we can develop new strategies for teaching students to use language effectively, which is the goal of this book.

✔ *Myth:*
BEGINNING WRITERS MUST MASTER THE PARTS OF SPEECH BEFORE THEY LEARN TO WRITE.

Memorizing terms and identifying parts of speech in practice exercises is not the same thing as knowing how to generate sentences that employ educated language conventions. Teaching students to write well requires much more sophisticated learning than merely parroting definitions. Mastering terminology is a skill that is best learned in conjunction with learning how to do something rather than as a prerequisite that is separate from the activity. Spending large amounts of class time circling and labeling words in isolated sentences leaves little time for meaningful writing instruction.

✔ Myth:

GRAMMAR INSTRUCTION IMPROVES WRITING.

In more than 90 years of educational research there has never been a single study that demonstrates a direct correlation between skills-based grammar instruction and improved writing performance. The work of Constance Weaver (see Chapter 10) provides more information on these studies. In contrast, our cultural expectations—held by parents, administrators, teachers, and students alike—are that another dose of grammar drills will cure any and all writing problems. Teaching writing would be much easier if this assumption were true.

✔ Myth:

MOST CHILDREN DO NOT UNDERSTAND GRAMMAR.

Young children exhibit elaborate, intuitive knowledge about sentence structure, including usage rules such as forming plurals and conjugating verbs. Children learn language by imitating adults. Children's ability to understand the parts of speech has been demonstrated with nonsense words. When told to match the tool, substance, and action form of the nonsense words: "a sib," "some sib," and "sibbing," researchers found that 3-year-olds could identify the

grammar forms successfully (Weaver, 1996). Everyone who can speak coherent sentences employs an understanding of language that far exceeds one's metacognitive awareness of these grammatical constructions. Students' intuitive understanding of language is a good starting point for school instruction.

Fact
WRITERS DO NEED GRAMMAR INSTRUCTION.

These misconceptions about grammar instruction do not mean that teachers should abandon the subject. Without grammar, our utterances would be little more than random groups of words. Grammar is a language system with predictable patterns. Patterns formulated as rules make us feel comfortable and safe in a world that is too often unpredictable. In fact, we actively create patterns in all areas of life: Sports statistics and even weather predictions are expressed with mathematical patterns; art and music are full of visual and sound patterns; and poetry and songs contain grammatical patterns.

The question then is not whether to teach grammar but which methods are the most effective. Instruction should match the brain's preferred cognitive-learning strategies. Imitation is the primary method that infants use to learn language. Babies imitate the patterns of facial expressions, gestures, sounds, words, and sentences without direct instruction. This knowledge can be called *intuitive* or *subconscious* because children do not know that they know it. The intuitive user can do the activity but cannot explain this knowledge explicitly or thoughtfully to someone else. One characteristic of learning by imitation is that at first the performance is more global or approximate. That is, the new learner imitates the most prominent features first and learns the smaller, more refined features last. This is why, for instance, educated adults are more concerned with the smaller features of language than children are. Tiny language errors such as misplaced modifiers can really irritate adults who are sophisticated language users, making it difficult for us to be patient with students' mistakes.

My process for teaching grammar is to move students from joyful, intuitive imitation to critical, conscious-level awareness of small language features during instruction and then to new, intuitive uses in everyday life. It can be difficult to introduce students to small linguistic features that run counter to their early language habits. Many of our language habits are dialect features that are part of our identities as members of families or communities that matter more to us than school or teachers. However, many people are masterful at the imitation of accents, dialects, and even the idiolects of well-known actors, politicians, and coworkers. It is possible to learn to speak and write in a different way if we have the motive and the understanding to do so.

Making the subconscious imitation of these patterns conscious can help students to gain better control of language. As they analyze imitated language patterns, students can become aware of what they know implicitly about grammar. Leading the class in metacognitive reflection about meaningful writing helps students recognize the grammar pattern on their own—I like to call these classroom discussions "wondering" about language. Thus, writing a poem, song, or rhyme comes first. Grammar is a teachable moment inside of a larger lesson about writing something significant to share with others. Since language is acquired best during meaningful communication acts in real life, writing a dummy exercise that ends up in the trash provides a weak opportunity for language instruction. Artistic publishing and sharing with others can make writing more significant to the author. You'll find ideas for implementing these language-learning principles in each chapter, so you can target a key grammar objective while providing students with a meaningful, memorable language experience.

TIP

Chapter 10 offers more in-depth research on learning and language instruction that can support you in developing new writing- and reading-based strategies for teaching grammar.

Cures for a Boring School Day

by Kalli Dakos

Invent a new toy.   1

Weigh cotton candy.   2

Go on an insect safari.   3

Write a letter to Donald Duck or Goofy.   4

Eat jellybean sandwiches and candy-apple soup.   5

Turn your classroom into a theater and act out poems.   6

Compete in the First Annual Bubble-Gum Blowing Olympics.   7

CHAPTER 2 **VERBS**

Cures for a Boring Day Poems

▱ ▱ ▱ ▱ ▱ ▱ **Instructional Objective:** ▱ ▱ ▱ ▱ ▱ ▱ ▱

Students write a "Cures for a Boring Day" poem that contains seven lines, each of which begins with a present-tense action verb.

Source Poem: "Cures for a Boring School Day" by Kalli Dakos (reproducible page 13)

Introductory Activity

Distribute copies of "Cures for a Boring School Day" by Kalli Dakos to the class. Have students read the poem chorally, with students on the right side of the room reading only the first word of each line and students on the left side of the room finishing the line. Reading the poem several times while adding dramatic vocal variations, sound effects, movements, level changes, and gestures will help students to internalize the grammar pattern.

Modeling Activity

Imitate the model poem using a new action. Begin by having students select an action that the author did not choose: make, draw, read, count, list, create, find, and so forth. For the class poem, all of the lines should begin with the same action word, for example, *make*. Have students individually brainstorm a list of fun but safe actions to do at school that can follow the chosen action word, such as "Make a bracelet out of paper clips," or "Make a class mascot sculpture out of paper wads." Then have them choose a favorite idea from their list, and on a large sticky note or index card, write their own poem line, starting with the selected action word. Ask for seven students to volunteer their lines for the class poem. Write down the seven lines on sentence

TIP

The purpose of the introductory activity is simply for students to imitate the pattern found in each line of the poem through expressive, repeated readings; wait to discuss grammar terminology until after the imitation exercise is over and students are able to consciously imitate the pattern.

14

strips, which you can set with sticky tack on the board or place in a pocket chart. Ask the class to suggest how to organize the lines from shortest to longest, as they appear in the model poem. Reorganize the lines accordingly to complete the class poem. Use the title "Cures for a Boring Day."

Place students in teams of seven to complete a group "Cures for a Boring Day" poem. Tell them to share their lines first, decide how they best fit together in terms of sense, sound, and length, and then revise and organize the lines so they move from shortest to longest. They can stick or tape the lines together when they're satisfied. One person in the group can be responsible for copying the poem. You can publish the class poems by posting them on a bulletin board in the cafeteria or study hall or including them in the school newsletter.

Grammar Mini-Lesson

Three ways to define action verbs are listed below. Consider which explanation will help your particular group of students learn the concept.

Question:
An action verb answers the question *What is the thing that happened?*

Meaning:
A verb expresses action. Verbs enable us to assert information about the things that we name. Research about inner speech has shown that we tend to think in terms of actions rather than in terms of who did the action because we usually know who did the action. Experienced writers select verbs carefully since they are so crucial to the meaning of a sentence.

Function:
An action verb describes what the subject does in a sentence. Verbs are essential to communication. You can sometimes drop the subject from a sentence but never the verb.

Have students examine the action verbs in the source poem (*invent, write, weigh, eat, compete, go,* and *turn*). Have a few students copy their sentences from the modeling activity on the overhead or the board as a quick way to add their writing into your explanation, and let the class identify the action verbs. There is no need to get too technical when you introduce the concept, though you may want to show students how to use the dictionary to find a word's part of speech. But ultimately, the true test is for students to identify how the word is used in context—the part of speech is determined by the word's function in a given sentence.

> **TIP**
>
> Using students' examples puts the grammar in a meaningful context for the class and garners more attention than textbook sentences—and students whose lines are used feel like stars.

Prewriting for an Individual Pattern Poem

Students can write their own "Cures for a Boring Day" poems. You may want to add to their topic choices by changing the setting from school to home or another appropriate place. Brainstorm a class list of possible "boring" settings: backyard, front steps, grocery store, library, church, car wash, Grandma's house, department store, fast food restaurant, barbershop, bank, and so forth.

Have students each select a place where they might find themselves bored. Tell students to jot down as many ideas as they can for entertaining actions that a person could do in this place, such as imaginary happenings, inventions from found materials, scientific experiments, interesting observations, arts and crafts creations, silly sporting events, fictional dramas, creative improvements, and activities with friends.

Writing the Poem

Have students draft their own poems, imitating the pyramid structure of the original model, with each line beginning with an action verb and containing more words or letters than the previous line. Draw the frame below for students to use as a guide.

TIP

Sharing an attractively published model poem written by you or a student before students start to write will heighten interest. Another motivational strategy is to announce the special audience or place selected for sharing or displaying the poems.

Cures for a Boring Day

_____.
(Action)   1

_____.
(Action)   2

_____.
(Action)   3

_____.
(Action)   4

_____.
(Action)   5

_____.
(Action)   6

_____.
(Action)   7

Publishing Activity

A to-do list format calls for a simple publishing solution. Provide students with attractive sheets of lined paper for publishing their "Cures for a Boring Day" poems. You might even use a real "Things to Do" pad of memo paper, giving each student one sheet for his or her poem, or have students create a "Things to Do" heading on the computer and use related clip art to decorate. Post students' poems in a local greeting card or stationery store.

Cures for a Boring Afternoon

Prepare an all-chocolate pizza,

Sing several nursery rhymes backwards,

Fashion a flowery hat for your grandma to wear,

Make musical instruments out of stuff from the kitchen,

Teach the dog to catch water balloons without breaking them,

Celebrate National Dental Week by decorating your toothbrush,

Converse with a neighbor using only words that begin with the letter *d.*

Metacognitive Moment

Select some of the thought teasers below that are appropriate for your students. Have students discuss their ideas in small groups and then share their responses with the whole class for further wondering and discussion.

- Name the subject or actor of Kalli Dakos's poem. (*The subject is the person who is the imagined reader of the list. In this case the subject is understood to be you, the reader. Each line is in the imperative or command form.*)

- List three situations in which someone might make up a list of commands. (*Possible answers: ways to entertain children when babysitting, what to do in case of a fire, how to make biscuits, and so forth.*)

- *Invent, weigh, go, write, eat, turn,* and *compete* are all verbs. Create an original definition for a verb that compares a verb to something else. (*Possible answers: a verb is like a video or DVD because it shows the action, or a verb is like a play-by-play sports announcer because it tells the action.*)

- This poem is a things-to-do list for today. Rewrite the list, making it a list of things that you did yesterday, following this pattern: *Invented a new toy.* (*Weighed cotton candy. Went on an insect safari. Wrote a letter to . . . . Ate jellybean sandwiches. Competed in the first. . . . Notice that three of these verbs are irregular and do not take an –ed ending for past tense:* went, wrote, *and* ate.)

- Decide what type of information is given after the verb. (*Most of the lines name a direct object, telling what thing the action affected; however, technically the third and last lines tell where something happened. Any information given about the action is part of the predicate of the sentence. Each line of the poem is a complete predicate.*)

TIP

The point of this type of discussion is to develop conceptual thought processes. Students are not being tested on the material; instead, they are encouraged to have the sort of conversation a group of linguists might have.

Grammar Reinforcement Activities

At this point students have encountered verbs through both reading and writing poetry, yet some students may need additional support. Use the following activities to reinforce the basic concept and provide an opportunity to discuss additional information or confusing features of verbs. Consider which of these suits the ability level of your students and the amount of class time you have available.

Analogy:
Superheroes make good subjects for action movies because they are always busy doing something. Superheroes can be compared to action verbs because of the activities that they do. Have students write a "Things to Do" list for their favorite superhero.

> **Superhero's Things-to-Do List:**
> ★ Fly faster than a speeding bullet.
> ★ Leap tall buildings with a single bound.
> ★ Stop a powerful locomotive.
> ★ Capture evil villains.
> ★ Stay away from Kryptonite.

Physical:
Start with a list of vivid verbs on filing cards. Have students play charades in teams by pantomiming action verbs. Or invite them to take turns using a toy superhero figure to perform the action verbs.

Grammar Extension Activity

An additional concept about verbs can be introduced to students who want to learn more, or this activity can be used for an extra-credit assignment.

Time:
Human beings are very concerned about time. Verbs indicate the time when the action occurred. The model poem format requires that students write their lines in present tense. Challenge students to write three diary entries for their superhero that specify past, present, and future actions. This is an effective way for students to see the differences between the three tenses.

Wonder Woman's Diary

Things I Did Yesterday:
★ Flew to the jungle
★ Deflected bullets from my enemies
   with my Amazon bracelets

Things to Do Today:
★ Trap the Nazi villains with my golden lasso.
★ Return the treasure to the rightful owners.

Things to Do Tomorrow:
★ I will polish my golden belt and
   silvery bracelets.
★ I will look for new red boots.

Topic Variations

You can change the assignment so that students write from a different perspective or for a different purpose. For example, students might write "Things to Do" poems about

- what cats do when they are bored.
- what tollbooth operators do when they are bored.
- ways to get bonus points from a teacher.
- ways to earn a raise in allowance.
- actions that a firefighter does.

Writing About Literature

Students can compose a "Cures for a Boring Day" poem based on the traits of a literary character:

- for the Troll from the classic fairy tale *The Three Billy Goats Gruff.*
- for brave Caddie from Carol Ryrie Brink's *Caddie Woodlawn.*

TIP

Practicing the poetic pattern for a character from a fairy tale, nursery rhyme, fable, or tall tale may help students to prepare for writing a poem about a novel.

📖 Brink, C. R. (1997). *Caddie Woodlawn.* New York: Aladdin Books.

📖 Carpenter, S. (1998). *The three billy goats gruff.* New York: HarperFestival.

What I Found in My Desk
by Bruce Lansky

A ripe peach with an ugly bruise,   1

a pair of stinky tennis shoes,   2

a day-old ham-and-cheese on rye,   3

a swimsuit that I left to dry,   4

a pencil that glows in the dark,   5

some bubble gum found in the park,   6

a paper bag with cookie crumbs,   7

an old kazoo that barely hums,   8

a spelling test I almost failed,   9

a letter that I should have mailed,   10

and one more thing, I must confess,   11

a note from teacher: Clean This Mess!!!!   12

Lost and Found Poems

¤ ¤ ¤ ¤ ¤ ¤ **Instructional Objective:** ¤ ¤ ¤ ¤ ¤ ¤ ¤

Students write a "Lost and Found" poem that contains at least one common noun in each line.

Source Poem: "What I Found in My Desk" by Bruce Lansky (reproducible page 20)

Introductory Activity

Distribute copies of "What I Found in My Desk" by Bruce Lansky to the class. Assign two students to each line so that you have a reader and a sound-effect partner. Have the class read the poem with the sound-effect partner making a sound to match the line. For example, for the first line a student might say, "Ouch" for the bruised peach. Have partners switch parts and have the class read the poem again.

Modeling Activity

Imitate the model poem using new lost and found items. Begin by having students brainstorm a few items that can be found in a messy person's desk or a locker, such as library books, permission forms, and CDs. When the class runs out of ideas, look back at Lansky's poem to review the types of things that he describes: food, sports equipment, school supplies, broken items, trash, and so forth. Have each student select a favorite item from the class list and, on a small piece of paper or sticky note, write a line that describes the item.

Select ten volunteers to write their lines with overhead markers onto two-inch strips cut from clear acetate or transparency sheets. Place the strips on the overhead projector and take suggestions from the class for the order of the lines. You can group similar items together or balance humorous items throughout the poem.

Use the author's last two lines to end the poem: "and one more thing, I must confess, a note from teacher: Clean This Mess!!!!" Add the title "What I Found in My Desk." Recopy the poem onto chart paper. You may want to publish the class poem by posting it on a bulletin board by the lost-and-found box or including it in the school newspaper.

Grammar Mini-Lesson

Three ways to define this concept are listed below. Consider which explanation will help your particular group of students learn the concept.

Question:
A noun answers the question *Who or what did the action?*

Meaning:
A noun names a person, place, thing, or idea. Learning the names of things or nouns comes first when acquiring a first or a second language. Naming the things in our universe is important to all human beings; what we cannot name, we cannot even think about. Experienced writers search for a more exact noun before adding adjectives.

Function:
A noun can be the subject or the object in a sentence or phrase. One way to test a word to see if it is a noun is to see if it can be possessed. Have students test words by using them to fill in the blank in this sentence: *I talked about my _____.*

Have students examine the nouns in the source poem (*peach, pencil, test, shoes, gum, letter, ham-and-cheese, bag, thing, swimsuit, kazoo, note, mess, bruise, dark, crumbs, pair, park, teacher,* and *rye*). Then have a few students copy their lines from the modeling activity on the overhead or the board as a quick way to add their writing into your explanation, and let the class identify the common nouns.

Prewriting for an Individual Pattern Poem

Students can write their own "Lost and Found" poems for things that they have found (real or imagined). Tell students to jot down as many ideas as they can for objects that could be lost or discarded, such as food, clothes, sports equipment, school supplies, snacks, broken items, assignments, trash, and unusual items.

Writing the Poem

Have students draft their own poems, imitating the list structure of the original model with each line beginning with the article *a* or *an* and containing a noun. Draw the frame below for students to use as a guide.

What I Found in My Locker

A/an _____ , (item)	1
a/an _____ , (item)	2
a/an _____ , (item)	3
a/an _____ , (item)	4
a/an _____ , (item)	5
a/an _____ , (item)	6
a/an _____ , (item)	7
a/an _____ , (item)	8
a/an _____ , (item)	9
a/an _____ , (item)	10
and one more thing, I must confess,	11
a note from teacher: Clean This Mess!!!!	12

Publishing Activity

An attractive, simple way for students to publish their "Lost and Found" poems is to create locker cards. Have students follow these directions:

1. Fold a sheet of construction paper in half like a greeting card. Then write your poem inside.

2. Decorate the front of the card with a drawing of a locker or desk.

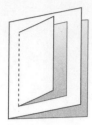

3. For an added effect, cut a flap in the front of the card that you can lift to reveal the poem. Cut the flap to create a "door" with a hinged opening: the front of the locker can fold open right to left or the top of the desk can lift from bottom to top. The cover edges can be glued to the back. This way the poem is revealed when the flap is lifted. Post students' poems in the hallway, lined up in rows like lockers.

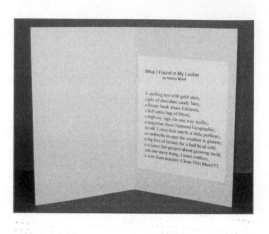

Metacognitive Moment

Select some of the thought teasers below that are appropriate for your students. Have students discuss their ideas in small groups and then share their responses with the whole class for further wondering and discussion.

• Most of the lines in Lansky's poem begin with the article *a*. Name the line that begins with *an* (*an old kazoo*). Find another noun phrase that begins with *an* (*an ugly bruise*). Look at the two example lines with *an* and explain the reason why these words take *an* and the others take *a*. (*An is used with words that begin with a vowel because it is difficult to pronounce two vowels together. For example, "a ugly bruise" sounds awkward.*)

• *Peach, swimsuit, pencil, gum,* and *bag* are all nouns. Create an original definition for a noun that compares a noun to something else. (*Possible answers: a noun is like a name tag because it tells the name of the thing, or a noun is like a catalog index because it tells what things are included.*)

• Some nouns are singular (one item) and some are plural (more than one item). Find the two nouns that are plural in this poem. (*The plural nouns are shoes and crumbs.*)

• List three situations in which you might make up a list of nouns. (*Possible answers: things that I want for my birthday, a camping list, and an inventory list for a store.*)

Grammar Reinforcement Activities

At this point students have encountered nouns through both reading and writing poetry, yet some students may need additional support. Use the following activities to reinforce the basic concept and provide an opportunity to discuss additional information or confusing features of nouns. Consider which of these mini-lessons suits the ability level of your students and the amount of class time you have available.

Analogy:
Using specific nouns is important for accuracy. If a magic genie were to grant you three wishes, you would need to be careful what you wish for. The noun *car* is not as specific as a brand name, such as *Corvette*. The noun *house* is not as specific as *mansion*. Pairs of students can make illustrated cards to represent vague and specific nouns for the same wish.

Physical:
Students can create name labels from sticky notes for common items in a classroom, such as desk, door, and clock, and post them on objects. If one of your students is an English language learner (ELL), he or she can write the names of the objects in his or her first language for a cultural exchange in your room.

Grammar Extension Activity

An additional concept about nouns can be introduced to students who want to learn more, or this activity can be used for an extra-credit assignment.

Proper and Common:
Catalog descriptions and advertisements list brand names that are capitalized. Share an advertisement with students and identify the proper and common nouns, calling attention to the capitalization of proper nouns. You might want students to practice substituting proper nouns in Lansky's poem. For example, they can add a brand name in place of shoes or bubble gum or include the place-name of the park (*some Juicy Fruit found in Dogwood Field*). Ask students why Lansky uses common nouns instead of proper nouns. (*One possible answer might be that common nouns make the poem appeal to a more general audience; without specifically naming the items found inside, this desk could belong to any kid.*)

Capitalization can be tricky for words like *grandma*. *Grandma* and other words for relatives are capitalized only when they are substituted for or paired with a person's name as in Grandma Jones. *Grandma* would not be capitalized in the phrase *a letter to my grandma*. Also, the word *park* can be capitalized if it is used as part of the name of a specific park, as in Great Smoky Mountains National Park. Challenge students to add three proper nouns to their poems.

Topic Variations

You can change the assignment to a different location. Students can write a "Lost and Found" poem about finding lost items

- at the dump.
- in a spy's briefcase.
- in an old cave.
- in a trunk in the attic.
- in an alien's spaceship.

Writing About Literature

Students can compose a "Lost and Found" poem about a place or object related to a literary character:

- for Snow White's cupboard from the classic fairy tale "Snow White and the Seven Dwarfs."

- for Claudia's backpack from E. L. Konigsburg's *From the Mixed-Up Files of Mrs. Basil E. Frankweiler.*

Heins, P. (Trans.) (1974). *Snow White by the Brothers Grimm.* Boston: Little, Brown.

Konigsburg, E. L. (1967). *From the mixed-up files of Mrs. Basil E. Frankweiler.* New York: Atheneum.

Encounter
by Lilian Moore

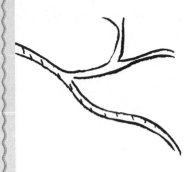

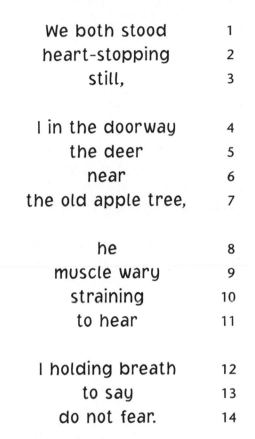

We both stood	1
heart-stopping	2
still,	3
I in the doorway	4
the deer	5
near	6
the old apple tree,	7
he	8
muscle wary	9
straining	10
to hear	11
I holding breath	12
to say	13
do not fear.	14
In the silence	15
between us	16
my thought said	17
Stay!	18
Did it snap	19
like a twig?	20
He rose on a curve	21
and fled.	22

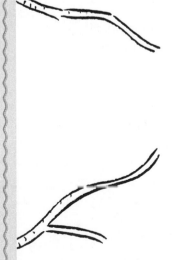

Encounter Poems

⌗ ⌗ ⌗ ⌗ ⌗ ⌗ **Instructional Objective:** ⌗ ⌗ ⌗ ⌗ ⌗ ⌗

Students write an "Encounter" with six stanzas, each containing at least one personal pronoun.

Source Poem: "Encounter" by Lilian Moore (reproducible page 27)

Introductory Activity

Distribute to each student a copy of "Encounter" by Lilian Moore. Assign two students to read the poem aloud: Both students read the first stanza together; student one reads stanzas two, four, and five (the narrator's part); and student two reads stanzas three and six (the deer's part). Have students read the poem again, this time with two additional students pantomiming the parts of the deer and the person.

Modeling Activity

Imitate the model poem using a new encounter. Begin by having students select a wild animal they would like to meet in a surprise encounter—a fox, squirrel, mouse, rabbit, or turtle, for example. Next, have students offer suggestions for how they might meet the animal, where the meeting might take place, their reaction and the animal's reaction, and the outcome of the meeting. For each stanza, have students brainstorm four or more ideas. Record them all on the overhead, board, or chart paper and then let the class vote on one to craft into a stanza. Lead the class in structuring the poem: Note that the first three stanzas begin with a pronoun (you may want to require that all stanzas begin with a pronoun to provide more structure for students) and that each stanza is written like a snapshot, capturing a moment in a brief span of time (*In the silence / between us / my thought said / Stay!*). If the stanzas are not written as discrete snapshot images or the poem doesn't read as a continuing narrative, rewrite the lines together, making sure that students can imitate the pattern. Since this poem's format is more complex than others in this book, students may need extra help imitating the stanza format. If so, have small groups of students write a second poem for another animal. You may want to publish the class poem by sending it to a local nature preserve or naturalist Web site for display.

Grammar Mini-Lesson

Three ways to define this concept are listed below. Consider which explanations will help your particular group of students learn the concept.

Question:
A pronoun serves as a substitute for a noun to prevent needless repetition. It answers the question *What word replaces a person's name or a noun?*

Meaning:
A pronoun names people, places, things, and ideas just the way a noun does, but it is less specific (*she* can refer to Mary and also to Jane). Pronouns are some of the most frequently used words in the English language since they serve as substitutes for nouns. Because we use them so often, we must be careful to make sure our readers know to what or to whom we're referring; if we use them carelessly, pronouns can make a reader confused about the people and things we're writing about.

Function:
A pronoun takes the place of a noun and acts like a noun, as the subject or object of a sentence or phrase. A pronoun must therefore match or agree with the specific noun that it replaces, the antecedent.

Have students examine the pronouns in the source poem (*we, he, my, I, us, it*) and ask them to identify the noun to which each pronoun refers. Then have them examine the class poem and identify the pronouns and their antecedents there as well.

Prewriting for an Individual Pattern Poem

Have students compose their own "Encounter" poems for a surprising meeting with an animal. As a class, brainstorm a list of animal categories, such as mammals, reptiles, fish, insects, birds, extinct and rare animals, and large and small animals.

Have each student select a favorite animal. Tell students to jot down as many ideas as they can for where they met, when they met, how they met, their reaction to the meeting, the animal's reaction to the meeting, and how the meeting ended.

Writing the Poem

Have students draft their poems, imitating the story structure of the original model, beginning each line with a pronoun, and including details about the meeting. Draw the frame below for students to use as a guide.

Encounter

We both_____. 1
(how and when the meeting took place)

I was_____. 2
(where)

It (s/he) was_____. 3
(where)

I_____. 4
(reaction)

It (s/he) _____. 5
(reaction)

It (s/he)_____. 6
(how the meeting ended)

Publishing Activity

The double-door folder makes a great display piece for students' "Encounter" poem. Have students follow these directions:

1. Start with an $8\frac{1}{2}$- by 14-inch sheet of cardstock paper. Position the paper horizontally. Fold the right and left sides of the paper to the center to form double doors over the middle of the paper.

2. On the left door, draw a self-portrait or glue a photo of yourself (the narrator) and on the right door, draw or glue a picture of the animal or person described in your poem. (Note: You may use clip art or a photograph of an animal printed from the Internet on the right side.)

3. Open the folding doors and write the poem in the center of the paper.

Send students' poems to be displayed at a local nature center or considered for publication in a kid's science or nature magazine like *Ranger Rick*. Or post the poems in a local pet store.

Metacognitive Moment

Select some of the thought teasers below that are appropriate for your students. Have students discuss their ideas in small groups and then share their responses with the whole class for further wondering and discussion.

- The author of this poem retells or narrates an incident that happened to the speaker. *I* is a first-person pronoun that is used to narrate an incident. When someone asks you what you did last weekend, it would be strange to use your name rather than the pronoun *I* to tell what you did. Try it: Name three things that you did on Saturday using your name as the subject. Then reword the same sentences with the pronoun *I*. (*Nancy woke up early. Nancy ate breakfast. Nancy went to a soccer game. I woke up early. I ate breakfast. I went to a soccer game.*)

- *We, both, I, he,* and *it* are all pronouns. Create an original definition for a pronoun that compares a pronoun to something else. (*Possible answers: a pronoun is like a substitute employee because it stands in for the regular staff [noun] or a pronoun is like an alias because it is another name for a noun.*)

- *I* is used twice in the model poem. Find another pronoun that refers to the speaker besides *I*. (*My is used in the fifth stanza.*) Identify what type of pronoun *my* is. (*My is a possessive pronoun because it shows ownership.*) Find another stanza that could have used *my* with another word. (*In the fourth stanza* my *could have been used with* breath.)

- A deer is an unusual sight. List three other unusual or remarkable nature sightings about which you would want to tell someone. (*Possible answers: spotting a rare bird, finding a bird's nest on the ground or an unhatched egg, or seeing a snake or a strange bug.*)

Grammar Reinforcement Activities

At this point students have encountered personal pronouns through reading and writing poetry, yet some students may need additional support. Use the following activities to reinforce the basic concept and provide an opportunity to discuss additional information or confusing features of pronouns. Consider which of these mini-lessons suits the ability level of your students and the amount of class time you have available.

Visual:

A pronoun must agree with the gender of the noun it replaces. Some animals have different names for the male and female of the species. Print the male and female columns below in a large font on transparency film. Cut out the individual animal names, and have students sort them by the male and female pronouns *He* and *She*.

Animal	He Male	She Female
Cattle	Bull	Cow
Chicken	Rooster	Hen
Deer	Buck	Doe
Duck	Drake	Duck
Fox	Dog	Vixen
Goose	Gander	Goose
Horse	Stallion	Mare
Lion	Lion	Lioness
Sheep	Ram	Ewe
Swine	Boar	Sow
Tiger	Tiger	Tigress

Physical:

Pronouns replace nouns so that a paragraph can flow smoothly rather than trip up readers with lots of repeated nouns. Copy the following paragraph on to the board or overhead and have a student read the paragraph aloud as it is written. For the second reading, have the student read any nouns that refer to people only once. Give three other students large name cards that say *They*, *She*, and *He*. When the reader comes to a repeated noun, the person with the pronoun card reads the pronoun replacement.

> Cinderella could leave for the ball only after the mean sisters were gone. The mean sisters thought that Cinderella would neither be able to get a dress nor find transportation in time to go to the ball. Just to be extra nasty, the mean sisters required Cinderella to do more chores. The mean sisters were anxious to meet the Prince. The Prince was very handsome, and the mean sisters hoped that the Prince would pick one of the mean sisters to wed.

Grammar Extension Activity

Two additional concepts about pronouns can be introduced to students who want to learn more, or these activities can be used for extra-credit assignments.

Possessives:
Pronouns can indicate ownership. In the example poem below, *my*, *its*, and *her* are possessive pronouns. In the third line, *her* is in the objective case and in line five *her* is possessive. Students can be asked to identify which use of the word *her* is possessive. Students can be challenged to add a possessive pronoun to their poems.

> **Encounter**
> We met
> at Wilkie's Bookstore
> last Thursday evening,
> I waited with my dad
> in the endless line
> for over an hour,
> She
> signed the title pages
> of each book placed in front of her.
> I silently handed over
> my copy
> with its worn and tattered cover,
> She
> smiled and winked
> when she saw
> how much I loved her story.
> She slid my book
> back across the table
> and thanked me for the compliment.

Case:
In the English language, nouns sometimes change form when they are used in a different case than their primary use. Pronouns often change form when they are moved from the subject position to the object position (usually at the end of the sentence). In the example poem above, *she* changed to *her* and *I* changed to *me*. Ask students how *we* and *it* change when moved to the objective case. (We *changes to* us *and* it *stays the same.*)

Topic Variations

You can change the assignment to include other people and fantasy beings. Students can write an "Encounter" poem about the narrator's meeting with

- a favorite movie star.
- a famous inventor.
- a person from current events.
- a ghost.
- King Kong.

Writing About Literature

Students can compose an "Encounter" poem about the conflicts between two literary characters:

- for *Goldilocks and the Three Bears*: Baby Bear encounters Goldilocks.
- for Phyllis Reynolds Naylor's *Shiloh*: Marty Preston encounters Shiloh.

📖 Aylesworth, J. (2003). *Goldilocks and the three bears*. New York: Scholastic.

📖 Naylor, P. R. (1991). *Shiloh*. New York: Atheneum.

I'm Talking Big!
by Colin McNaughton

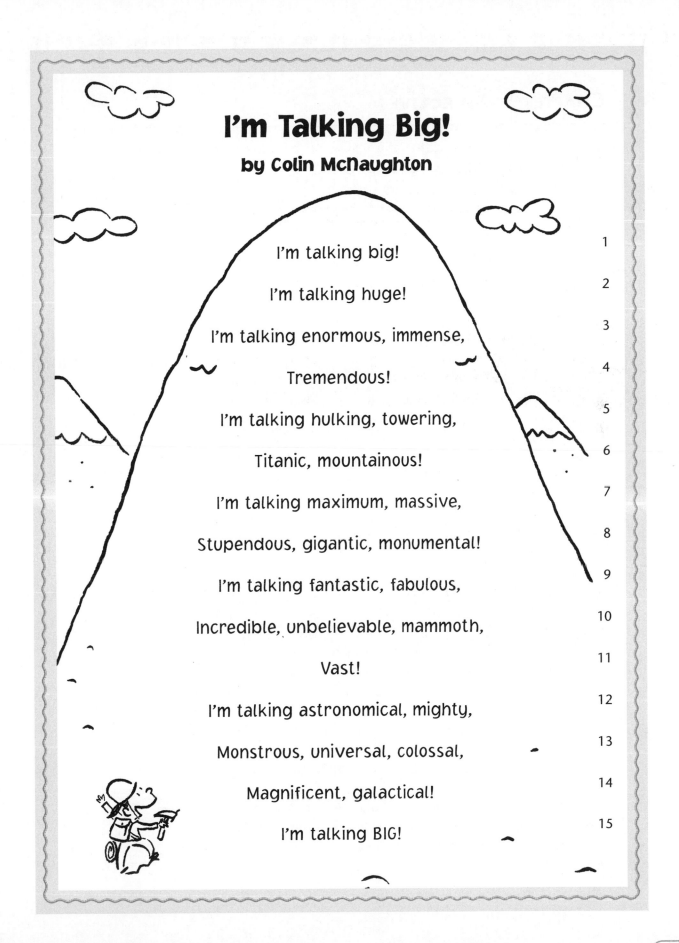

I'm talking big! 1

I'm talking huge! 2

I'm talking enormous, immense, 3

Tremendous! 4

I'm talking hulking, towering, 5

Titanic, mountainous! 6

I'm talking maximum, massive, 7

Stupendous, gigantic, monumental! 8

I'm talking fantastic, fabulous, 9

Incredible, unbelievable, mammoth, 10

Vast! 11

I'm talking astronomical, mighty, 12

Monstrous, universal, colossal, 13

Magnificent, galactical! 14

I'm talking BIG! 15

CHAPTER 5 **ADJECTIVES**

Synonym Poems

> ◻ ◻ ◻ ◻ ◻ ◻ **Instructional Objective:** ◻ ◻ ◻ ◻ ◻ ◻
>
> Students write a "Synonym" poem that contains 15 or more adjectives.
>
> Source Poem: "I'm Talking Big!" by Colin McNaughton (reproducible page 35)

Introductory Activity

Distribute copies of "I'm Talking Big!" by Colin McNaughton to the class. Assign each student to read aloud one or two of the 28 adjectives—two of which are *big* and the rest of which are synonyms for *big*. To read the poem as a class, you read the beginning of each sentence (*I'm talking . . .*) and have students chime in with their adjectives to complete the line. Have students read the poem again, this time trying to read faster and faster without anyone missing his or her part. For fun, you can have students rearrange the adjectives, asking them to read them in alphabetical order or from least number of letters to most.

Modeling Activity

Imitate the model poem using a new adjective. Begin by having students select a common adjective such as *small*, *good*, or *happy*. Brainstorm a list of synonyms for the chosen adjective on the overhead, board, or chart paper. Write each synonym on a clear slip of acetate (for the overhead) or a large sticky note (for the board or chart paper). Arrange the words into lines so that each successive line expands by one synonym. Take suggestions from the class for the order of the words and lines. Repeat the first line for the title and last line.

The class poem makes a rich vocabulary lesson. You might share the poem with another class, parent, or teacher who can be invited to return the favor by writing a similar poem, using an equal number of synonyms.

Grammar Mini-Lesson

Three ways to define these concepts are listed below. Consider which explanation to include in your plans for use with your particular students.

Question:
An adjective describes by answering the questions *What kind? Which one? How much? How many?*

Meaning:
Adjectives add descriptive information so that the speaker can be more precise about the people, places, things, and ideas in his or her writing. Adjectives clarify or distinguish one thing from another.

Function:
Adjectives modify nouns or pronouns. Adjectives often are placed in front of nouns but can be placed in other positions, as well, such as after a linking or state of being verb (*The object looked enormous* or *The object was enormous*). One way to test a word to see if it is an adjective is to place the word *very* in front of it.

Have students use one of the strategies above to identify all the adjectives in McNaughton's poem or in a favorite descriptive passage from a novel. The adjectives they'll find in the poem are *big, huge, enormous, immense, tremendous, hulking, towering, titanic, mountainous, maximum, massive, stupendous, gigantic, monumental, fantastic, fabulous, incredible, unbelievable, mammoth, vast, astronomical, mighty, monstrous, universal, colossal, magnificent,* and *galactical.*

Prewriting for an Individual Pattern Poem

Students can compose their own "Synonym" poems for a common adjective of their choice. As a class, brainstorm a list of common adjectives such as *angry, beautiful, tired, new, old, nice, mean, wet, dry, clean, dirty, hot, cold, heavy, stinky, greedy, rich,* and *poor.* Have each student select a favorite common adjective. Tell students to jot down as many synonyms as they can for their adjective. Encourage students to list words with few or many letters, and words ending with the letters *-ous, -able, -al, -ic,* or *-ing.* Students can look up their common adjective in the thesaurus to gather even more word choices.

Writing the Poem

Have students draft their own poems, imitating the stair-step structure of the original model with each line beginning with "I'm talking" and containing one more synonym than the line before. Draw the frame below for students to use as a guide.

I'm Talking _____**!**
               (descriptive word)

I'm talking _____!   1
           (descriptive word)

I'm talking _____!   2
           (synonym)

I'm talking _____, _____!   3
           (synonym) (synonym)

I'm talking _____, _____, _____!   4
           (synonym) (synonym) (synonym)

I'm talking _____, _____, _____, _____!   5
           (synonym) (synonym) (synonym) (synonym)

I'm talking _____, _____, _____, _____, _____!   6
           (synonym) (synonym) (synonym) (synonym) (synonym)

I'm talking _____!   7
           (descriptive word)

Remember to repeat the first line for line 7.

Publishing Activity

Students can write their "Synonym" poems in a fan book, a mini-book that opens like a fan to reveal each line on a strip. Have students follow these directions:

1. Cut eight 2-inch-wide strips from two sheets of standard paper, along the $8\frac{1}{2}$-inch side. Punch a hole in the center of the left side of each strip.

2. Write your poem, using one strip of paper for each line.

3. Decorate the completed poem by illustrating or making a simple border around each strip.

4. Arrange the lines of your poem in order, placing the strips in a stack with the holes aligned. Fasten the strips with a large brad to create the book. Now, as you read your poem, fan out the pages, strip by strip.

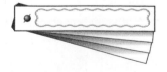

TIP

Have students write the longest line of their poems first to determine a script size that will fit on the strip. Remind them that their handwriting size will need to be small enough to fit all of the words of the longest line on a strip.

Ask students to make two copies of their poems, one to keep and one to give to a younger student, who can use the book like a thesaurus when he or she writes.

Metacognitive Moment

Select some of the thought teasers below that are appropriate for your students. Have students discuss their ideas in small groups and then share their responses with the whole class for further wondering and discussion.

- Count the number of commas that McNaughton uses in his poem. (*McNaughton uses 20 commas in his poem.*) Explain how these commas help the reader to understand the meaning. (*The commas separate the descriptions into equal units.*)

- *Big, huge,* and *enormous* are adjectives. Create an original definition for an adjective that compares it to something else. (*Possible answers: an adjective is like a police all-points bulletin because it identifies someone or something, or like a compliment or an insult because it describes someone or something in a positive or negative way.*)

- The author uses the phrase *I'm talking* as a way to start each line, which creates a concise way to grab the reader's attention at the beginning of each sentence. Suggest another way to begin McNaughton's sentences that would say the same thing but use more words. (*The author could have used* Let me tell you about something that is *or* I mean that this thing was really. *The phrase* I'm talking *is slang—it helps establish the rhythm and excited tone of the poem.*)

- List four different contexts in which adjectives could be used effectively. (*Possible answers: a product advertisement, a love letter, a travel brochure, comments on a report card, a counselor's records.*)

Grammar Reinforcement Activities

At this point students have encountered adjectives through both reading and writing poetry, yet some students may need additional support. Use the following activities to reinforce the basic concept and provide an opportunity to discuss additional information or confusing features of adjectives. Consider which of these mini-lessons suits the ability level of your students and the amount of class time you have available.

Visual:

Invite students to be adjective designers. Have each student start with an outline, die-cut shape, or clip-art image of an object such as a dog, car, dress, boat, ice cream cone, pizza slice, person, or spaceship. Tell students that they are to play the role of designer and change the look of one or more of the common objects by drawing in details. For example, a student could design five types of ice cream flavors. Then, using adjectives, the student would write the names of the new designs below each object. Ice cream flavors, for example, might be *scrumptious strawberry ice cream* or *bodacious blueberry ice cream*. You can also use images of popular media figures such as Elvis Presley or Selena, with students drawing the wardrobe and accessories to make their characters appear studious, punk, domestic, and so forth.

Physical:

Have students play a 20-question adjective guessing game. Cut out pictures of specific items that can be found in popular magazines such as food, furniture, or electronic products. Group students in teams of three and give each team a chance to guess an item. On a team's turn, show the picture to the rest of the class. Then hide the picture and let the team begin to ask questions using adjectives that will help them guess the object (have team members take turns asking questions). For example, students might ask *Is the item very* _____ ? (This format employs the "very" test for adjectives.)

Assign one student in the class to count the number of questions asked by the group, with 20 being the limit. Each group can guess the object in the picture only once. Ten points are scored for every correct guess, and the highest scoring team wins.

Grammar Extension Activity

An additional concept about adjectives can be introduced to students who want to learn more, or this activity can be used for an extra-credit assignment.

Suffixes:

One of the ways that a word can be turned into another part of speech is to add a suffix, or specific group of letters, to the end of a word. In fact, many of our suffixes come from other languages like Latin and Greek and have meanings that tell how they modify the word to which they are added. The chart on page 41 lists some common suffixes, their meanings, example words, and the literal meanings of these words.

Adjective-Forming Suffixes			
suffix	**meaning**	**example**	**literal meaning**
–ous	characterized by	enormous	characterized by enormity or hugeness
		tremendous	characterized by tremors or shaking
		mountainous	characterized by mountains
		stupendous	characterized by wonder or awe
		fabulous	characterized by fables or unbelievability
		monstrous	characterized by monsters
–able or –ible	able to	unbelievable	not able to be believed or confident about
		incredible	not able to be credited or possible
–al	pertaining to	monumental	pertaining to a monument or a building or statue
		astronomical	pertaining to astronomy or the stars
		universal	pertaining to the universe or one world
		colossal	pertaining to a colossus, a great statue of ancient times
–ic	being like	galactical	pertaining to the galaxy or Milky Way
		titanic	being like a titan or son of a mythological god
		gigantic	being like a giant or enemy of a mythological god
		fantastic	being like a fantasy or image or idea

These suffixes are similar in meaning since they all serve the function of turning words into adjectives. Notice that *astronomical* and *galactical* have two suffixes: *-ic* and *-al*. Some of our most sophisticated and technical words are created with prefixes and suffixes. Challenge students to add three words with suffixes to their poems or identify the words with suffixes that they are already using.

Topic Variations

You can change the assignment to replace some of the adjectives with simile phrases. Students can write a "Synonym" poem about the following topics, adding similes for a fun challenge:

● a sensation. Synonyms for *stinky* include *offensive, horrid, repulsive.* Simile: *as repulsive as a three-year-old tennis shoe.*

● an athlete. Synonyms for *fast* include *hypersonic, nimble, speedy.* Simile: *as speedy as students leaving on the last day of school.*

● a fashion advertisement. Synonyms for *popular* include *fashionable, stylish, famous.* Simile: *as famous as a top-of-the-charts band.*

● a restaurant. Synonyms for *tasty* include *delicious, savory, mouthwatering.* Simile: *as mouthwatering as the first strawberries of summer.*

● a vacation destination. Synonyms for *exciting* include *sensational, thrilling, breathtaking.* Simile: *as breathtaking as the aurora borealis.*

Writing About Literature

Students can compose a "Synonym" poem about the traits of a literary character:

● for Paul Bunyan's strength from his tall-tale adventures.

● for Lyddie's helpfulness to others even though she was quite poor herself, from Katherine Paterson's *Lyddie.*

Osborne, M. P. (1991). "Paul Bunyan" in *American Tall Tales.* New York: Knopf

Paterson, K. (1994). *Lyddie.* New York: Penguin Puffin.

Rebound

by Nancy Mack

Desperately, the ball is elbowed down,   1
    Finding one player free.   2

Gently, an airborne ball slides over the rim,   3
    Igniting frenzied fans.   4

Expectantly, eyes are riveted to the clock,   5
    While seconds are slowly counted.   6

Finally, the buzzer blares its signal,   7
    Terminating the tournament game.   8

Jubilantly, spectators pour from the stands,   9
As the shooter is happily hoisted upon shoulders.   10

Poetry in Motion

☒ ☒ ☒ ☒ ☒ ☒ **Instructional Objective:** ☒ ☒ ☒ ☒ ☒ ☒

Students will write a "Motion" poem that contains five or more adverbs.

Source Poem: "Rebound" by Nancy Mack   (reproducible page 43)

Introductory Activity

Distribute copies of "Rebound" by Nancy Mack to the class. Assign particular students to each line and have them read the poem aloud. Have students read the poem again, this time in the voice of an enthusiastic sports announcer. For fun, pass around a plastic, echo microphone (or even a rolled-up magazine) for each reader to use. Students can dramatize the action.

Modeling Activity

Imitate the model poem for a different sports event. Begin by having the class vote on a sport topic, such as football, soccer, or baseball, and then brainstorm a list of exciting events that take place during the game. Select one of these events for the class poem. Next brainstorm a list of adverbs, which you might simply introduce as "words ending in -*ly*," that describe the event. (If students know how to use the thesaurus and need extra support, you may want to let them look up synonyms for the adverbs listed and add a few to the class list.) Have each student select a favorite adverb and write two paired lines about the event: one beginning with a word ending in -*ly* and one beginning with a word ending in -*ing*, as in the poem.

Have students form groups of five to pool their lines and create a group poem. Begin by having students read their lines aloud and then arrange the lines in a logical order. Students should explain their reasons for the sequence they've chosen. Have the writers of each group stand, arrange themselves in order of the lines they've written, and read their poem to the class with each student speaking his or her part. Invite a local coach in to hear their poems. Poems can be written on stationery with sports graphics.

Grammar Mini-Lesson

Three ways to define adverbs are listed below. Consider which explanation will help your particular group of students learn the concept.

Question:
An adverb describes the action by answering the questions *When? Where? How?* and *To what degree?*

Meaning:
Adverbs show how the action was done by adding exactness or intensity. Skillful writers often try to strengthen a weak verb before they add an adverb.

Function:
Adverbs can modify many types of words: verbs, adjectives, and other adverbs. When modifying verbs, adverbs tell when, where, how, and to what degree. When modifying adjectives and other adverbs, adverbs indicate degree and usually intensify the word that is modified (*very* in *very nice* and *very quickly*). Adverbs are highly mobile and can appear almost anywhere in a sentence—before or after the verb and at the beginning and the end of a sentence. Adverbs indicating time often occur as the first word in a sentence, as in the following example: *Eventually, she changed her mind.* Adjectives and adverbs are hard to tell apart since some words can function as both. Many adverbs can be tested by placing them after an action verb in a sentence such as *Mickey reacted_____* and seeing whether the word describes when, where, how, or to what degree the action was done. Similarly, many adjectives can be tested by placing them after a linking verb in a sentence such as: *Mickey seemed_____* and seeing whether the word describes Mickey.

Have students use one of the above strategies to examine the adverbs in the source poem or in their own group poems. The adverbs in "Rebound" are *desperately, gently, expectantly, slowly, finally, jubilantly,* and *happily.*

Prewriting for an Individual Pattern Poem

Students can compose their own "Motion" poems for a sport of their choice. As a class, brainstorm a list of sports, games, hobbies, and athletic events. Be sure to include Olympic sports, board and card games, and popular pastimes like skateboarding, dancing, and marching band. Have each student select a favorite competitive activity. Tell students to jot down as many ideas as they can about their sport, such as equipment, terms for moves or positions, and exciting moments during play. Have students describe how the event starts, what incidents happen next, how the participants move or act, and how the crowd reacts. Ask students to list five *-ly* adverbs that could describe the actions they've listed.

Writing the Poem

Have students draft their own poems, imitating the paired line structure of the original model with the first line beginning with an *-ly* adverb and the second line beginning with an *-ing* action word. Draw the frame below for students to use as a guide.

(Name of the Activity)

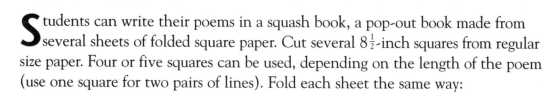

_____, the _____,   1
(*-ly* adverb)   (sentence about the action)

_____ _____.   2
(*-ing* action word)   (continues the action)

_____, the _____,   3
(*-ly* adverb)   (sentence about the action)

_____ _____.   4
(*-ing* action word)   (continues the action)

_____, the _____,   5
(*-ly* adverb)   (sentence about the action)

_____ _____.   6
(*-ing* action word)   (continues the action)

_____, the _____,   7
(*-ly* adverb)   (sentence about the final action)

_____ _____.   8
(*-ing* action word)   (continues the final action)

Publishing Activity

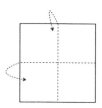

Students can write their poems in a squash book, a pop-out book made from several sheets of folded square paper. Cut several $8\frac{1}{2}$-inch squares from regular size paper. Four or five squares can be used, depending on the length of the poem (use one square for two pairs of lines). Fold each sheet the same way:

1. Fold the square in half, top to bottom, carefully matching the sides and heavily creasing the fold. Open the square and fold in half the other way, side to side.

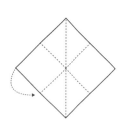

2. Open the square, and flip it over (this is a very important step!). Fold the square diagonally, corner to corner, making sure to line up the sides and crease heavily. (Note: Make only one diagonal fold.)

3. Open the square again and push the center point with your finger to turn the square inside out, folding the diagonal lines inward to form a smaller folded square; crease the folded square on all folds.

4. When you have folded all the squares you need, glue one square to the next square, overlapping quadrants as shown and making sure each square faces the opposite direction (one center points out and the next points in). Use a glue stick or small amounts of glue.

5. When the glue has dried, spread the book out vertically in front of you. Write each two-line stanza in the middle diamonds where the squares overlap. Decorate the side sections with stickers, drawings, or magazine clippings of sports visuals. The top and bottom of the folded book can be reinforced by gluing on slightly larger cardboard squares. On top of these you can glue circles cut in the shape of a large ball and then decorate them. Glue ribbon or yarn under the cardboard covers to tie the book closed.

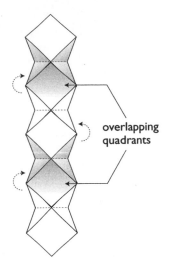

overlapping
quadrants

These squash books can be displayed at field day, a local sporting goods store, or a sports facility or arena.

Metacognitive Moment

Select some of the thought teasers below that are appropriate for your students. Have students discuss their ideas in small groups and then share their responses with the whole class for further wondering and discussion.

● List the seven adverbs in this poem and find the matching verb for each adverb. (*The adverb-verb pairs are desperately elbowed, gently slides, expectantly riveted, slowly counted, finally blares, jubilantly pour, and happily hoisted.*)

● Notice that each pair of lines forms a complete sentence. The author uses an adverb to begin each sentence. Can adverbs appear in places other than at the beginning of a sentence? See if you can rewrite this kernel sentence from the poem, putting *jubilantly* in another place: *Jubilantly, spectators pour from the stands.* Do the other adverbs in the poem work as well when they are moved from their position as the first word in the sentence? (*The adverb can be placed before or after the verb or at the end of the sentence. Not all of the other sentences make sense with the adverb moved to these three slots. For example, The buzzer blares finally its signal is an awkward construction.*)

- Give the most typical location for the adverb in a sentence. (*The most common location for an adverb is right in front of the verb. For example,* Spectators jubilantly pour from the stands.)

- Adverbs can tell when, where, or how something is done. Classify all of the adverbs in the poem into one of these three categories. (*The largest category is the "how" or "manner" category and includes* desperately, gently, expectantly, slowly, jubilantly, *and* happily. *There are no words for the "where" category, and only* finally *fits into the "when" category.*)

- Most adverbs that end in *-ly* tell the manner in which something is done. Rewrite the adverbs in the poem without their *-ly* suffix and create a sentence that uses each of the shortened words. Tell what part of speech you think these words are without their *-ly* endings. (*Desperate, gentle, expectant, slow, final, jubilant,* and *happy can act as adjectives. However,* final *can also be a noun. A possible sentence:* He was desperate to rebound the ball. *By adding and subtracting suffixes, we can increase the versatility of a word to function as other parts of speech.*)

- *Desperately, gently,* and *expectantly* are adverbs. Create an original definition for an adverb that compares it to something else. (*Possible answers: an adverb is like a fitness video because it explains how to do the action, or like a dance choreographer because it explains where, when, and how to move.*)

- List three different contexts in which adverbs could be used effectively. (*Possible answers: a track coach's directions, a discipline referral, and an eyewitness testimony.*)

Grammar Reinforcement Activities

At this point students have encountered adverbs through both reading and writing poetry, yet some students may need additional support. Use the following activities to reinforce the basic concept and provide an opportunity to discuss additional information or confusing features of adverbs. Consider which of these mini-lessons suits the ability level of your students and the amount of class time you have available.

Analogy:
Adverbs are like a radio sports announcer because they tell about the action, detailing when, where, and how the action took place. In fact, a sports announcer uses adverbs to paint a vivid picture of an event; without accurate adverbs the listening fans would not know what had just happened. You might tell students to hear the voice of a sports announcer in their minds when they need to use adverbs ("The coach watches attentively, anxiously, and apprehensively as Adrienne sprints adeptly, adroitly, and agilely into the end zone!").

Physical:
Have students play a pantomime game called Bowling for Adverbs. Write adverbs on slips of paper. Create teams of three or more players. Each team member selects an adverb and, without showing the word to his or her teammates, pantomimes bowling in the way the adverb describes. For example, if a student draws the adverb *nervously*, he or she might walk and hold the ball in a way that suggests anxiousness. The other team members work together to name the adverb in three guesses. Guessing the correct adverb on the first try is a strike (10 points), and guessing correctly in two or three guesses equals a spare (5 points).

The group may take three guesses to identify the adverb and then they must try a new adverb. The object is to guess accurately and quickly. The group with the most points at the end of the session wins.

Grammar Extension Activity

An additional concept about adjectives can be introduced to students who want to learn more, or this activity can be used for an extra-credit assignment.

Comparative and Superlative:
Similar to adjectives, adverbs can be comparative or superlative. Most adverbs that end in *-ly* take the word *more* in front of them to compare two items and *most* to explain a relationship among three or more items. A few adverbs can take the suffix *-er* to form a comparative and *-est* to form a superlative. Look at this chart, which gives comparative and superlative forms for example adverbs.

Comparative and Superlative Adverbs		
Adverb	**Comparative**	**Superlative**
slowly	more slowly	most slowly
gently	more gently	most gently
quickly	more quickly	most quickly
late	later	latest
early	earlier	earliest

Challenge students to rewrite one of their stanzas, adding a comparative or superlative adverb.

Topic Variations

You can change the assignment to focus on any type of activity. Students can write "Poetry in Motion" about

- pastimes during a particular season of the year.
- weather events like the first snow or heavy fog.
- a bargain hunter shopping for clothes or a new car.
- a bank robbery.
- a famous chef preparing a special dessert.

Writing About Literature

Students can compose a "Motion" poem about a climactic event in a story:

- for the wolf's discovery in *Little Red Riding Hood*.
- for the church burning in Christopher Paul Curtis's *The Watsons Go to Birmingham—1963*.

📖 Curtis, C. P. (1995). *The Watsons Go to Birmingham—1963*. New York: Delacorte.

📖 Grimm, J. L. & W. K. (1984). *Little Red Riding Hood*. New York: Holiday House.

Last Night I Dreamed of Chickens

by Jack Prelutsky

Last night I dreamed of chickens,   1

there were chickens everywhere,   2

they were standing on my stomach,   3

they were nesting in my hair,   4

they were pecking at my pillow,   5

they were hopping on my head,   6

they were ruffling up their feathers   7

as they raced about my bed.   8

They were on the chairs and tables,   9

they were on the chandeliers,   10

they were roosting in the corners,   11

they were clucking in my ears,   12

there were chickens, chickens, chickens   13

for as far as I could see. . . .   14

when I woke today, I noticed   15

there were eggs on top of me.   16

Dream Poems

> ¤ ¤ ¤ ¤ ¤ ¤ **Instructional Objective:** ¤ ¤ ¤ ¤ ¤ ¤
>
> Students write a "Dream" poem that contains ten or more prepositional phrases.
>
> Source Poem: "Last Night I Dreamed of Chickens" by Jack Prelutsky (reproducible page 51)

Introductory Activity

Distribute copies of "Last Night I Dreamed of Chickens" by Jack Prelutsky to the class. The first time through, read aloud the poem with the class, call-and-response style: You read the first part of each line, which contains the subject and simple predicate (*they were standing . . .*), and students read the second part, which contains the prepositional phrase (*. . . on my stomach*). For the second reading, group students in pairs and assign one line (numbers 2–13) to each pair. Have students practice reading the line with one partner reading the first part and the other partner reading the second part and using his or her hand as a puppet to dramatize the silly chicken actions. For example, for line 5, the partner reading "at my pillow" can make a pecking gesture at an imaginary pillow on the desk. (You may also want to let students use a stuffed chicken toy, a die cut of a chicken shape, or a rubber chicken to pass from pair to pair as students read and perform their lines.) When they're ready, start the poem off by reading the first line and then let the pairs read their assigned lines in order. For a third, more fluent reading, you may want to have pairs switch parts and read the whole poem through together. This activity should get lots of laughs.

Modeling Activity

Imitate the model poem using a new animal, with each student contributing a line to the poem. Begin by voting on an animal that will be the focus of the poem. Have each student sketch the animal onto a sheet of blank paper. (You can also use a rubber stamp, stickers, or a die-cut shape of the animal.) Suggest that students place the image somewhere other than in the center of the paper.

Provide a list of prepositions for students to use for this activity:

about	beneath	in	over
above	beside	inside	under
across	between	near	up
among	by	of	upon
at	down	on	
behind	from	outside	

Next, brainstorm a list of specific locations for the animal, using prepositions to start the phrase, such as *by the tree* and *under the bridge*. Have students draw the background for their prepositional phrase idea. Then have students write a phrase that tells where (*in the bathroom sink!*), using large print across the bottom of their page.

Use students' work to write a full poem on chart paper, starting with "Last night we dreamed of . . ." Have each student present his or her idea with an action (*They were [It was] jumping on the bed.*) and record the lines following the model poem format. Ask the class to collaborate on the last lines, which can be about objects left behind by the animal or about never again eating strange foods before bedtime. (*When I woke up today, I shook my head and firmly said / that I will never eat artichoke ice cream again before bed.*)

Hang the poem in a place where students can see it easily so they can refer to it during the grammar mini-lesson and when they write their own poems. The individual pages can be gathered together and bound into a picture book that can be shared with a younger class or put on display in a craft store where rubber stamps or stickers are sold.

Grammar Mini-Lesson

Three ways to define this concept are listed below. Consider which explanation will help your particular group of students understand the concept.

Question:
A preposition connects a noun or pronoun to another word that it modifies. A prepositional phrase can answer the questions *Where is it? When did it happen? How much? Which one? How is it similar?*

> **TIP**
>
> Since the point of the modeling activity is to imitate the grammar element rather than the sound element, it's not necessary that the lines of the class poem rhyme. Students can attempt rhyme later for extra credit in their individual poems.

Meaning:

Prepositions precede nouns or pronouns. The word *preposition* literally means "placed before." Prepositions are frequently matched with specific words, so prepositional phrases are idiomatic, or unique to a dialect, which makes them tricky for both native and ELL writers. (*We are in the habit **of** using a particular preposition, not in the habit **with** using a particular preposition.*) Although there are approximately 60 prepositions, we tend to use only 9 frequently: *of, on, to, at, by, for, from, in,* and *with*. Since prepositional phrases express relationships in space, time, and between things, these wonderful phrases help us to describe precisely and imaginatively, as with similes. (*Her enthusiasm was infectious, like a cold that we all began to catch.*) Intermediate writers learn to use prepositional phrases to include more information.

Function:

A prepositional phrase modifies another word in a sentence and is made up of a preposition and a noun or pronoun plus any modifying words. This descriptive phrase functions like an adjective when it modifies a noun or like an adverb when it modifies a verb. Prepositional phrases usually can be placed in more than one position in a sentence.

Using the class poem or the model poem, have students identify the prepositional phrases. You might have them circle each phrase in a color to show its location—the pattern will show that the phrases fall at the end of the sentence. You may also want to highlight in a different color the preposition that begins each phrase. The prepositional phrases in the source poem are:

of chickens	up their feathers	in my ears
on my stomach	about my bed	on top
in my hair	on the chairs and tables	of me
at my pillow	on the chandeliers	
on my head	in the corners	

Prewriting for an Individual Pattern Poem

Have students write their own "Dream" poems for an animal of their choice. As a class, brainstorm a list of possible animals. Consider several categories: mammals, reptiles, fish, insects, birds, extinct and rare animals, large and small animals, and fantasy animals. Have each student select a favorite animal. Tell students to jot down as many ideas as they can for strange places for their dream animal to be, such as unexpected places, hidden places, bothersome places, their neighborhoods, other cities, other countries, and geographic locations (mountains, beaches, deserts, polar regions, jungles, oceans, and outer space).

Writing the Poem

As students draft their own poems, encourage them to imitate the repeating line structure of the original model so that they open with *Last night I dreamed of _____*, and each line that follows begins with *They were* or *There were* and contains an *-ing* action word and a prepositional phrase showing where. Draw the frame below for students to use as a guide.

Last Night I Dreamed of _____
                    (animals)   1

Last night I dreamed of_____,
                   (animals)   2

there were _____ everywhere,
       (animals)   3

they were _____ _____,
     (*-ing* action word) (place phrase)   4

they were _____ _____,
     (*-ing* action word) (place phrase)   5

they were _____ _____,
     (*-ing* action word) (place phrase)   6

they were _____ _____,
     (*-ing* action word) (place phrase)   7

They were _____,
     (place phrase)   8

they were _____,
     (place phrase)   9

they were _____,
     (place phrase)   10

they were _____,
     (place phrase)   11

there were _____, _____, _____
     (animals)   (animals) (animals)   12

for as far as I could see. . . .

when I woke today, I noticed   13

there were _____ _____. 14
     (objects left by animals) (place phrase)   15

Publishing Activity

Students can publish their "Dream" poems in a shoebox made to look like a bed. Have students collect an average-sized shoebox or tissue box and follow these directions:

1. Cover the lid or top with a "blanket"—a piece of fabric or paper cut to drape over and reach the bottom of the two long sides of the box.

2. Cut a headboard and footboard out of brown cardboard. Tape the headboard and footboard to the ends of the box or attach with brads, leaving the top fourth loose for the lid of the box to slide down between the cardboard end pieces.

3. Fold a paper towel into thirds, stuff with another paper towel and staple or glue shut for a pillow and attach to the lid.

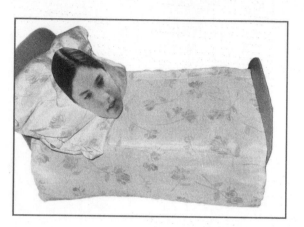

4. Make the dreaming person's head from a cardboard circle. Glue on a digital photo of the student's face or draw a face with markers and glue on yarn for hair.

5. Print out or write the poem as a four-page booklet, making sure that the pages are the right size to fit into the box (approximately 8½ by 5 inches). Print the title and author on the cover page, each stanza on a separate page, and the ending two lines on the last page. Place the poem inside of the box. These "Dream" poem beds can be displayed in a local furniture or department store.

Metacognitive Moment

Select some of the thought teasers below that are appropriate for your students. Have students discuss their ideas in small groups and then share their responses with the whole class for further wondering and discussion.

• Prepositions are used so frequently in sentences that we hardly notice them. Find the prepositions that Jack Prelutsky uses in his poem more than once. (*Prelutsky uses* on, in, *and* of *more than once.*)

• Prepositional phrases can have two or more words. Determine the most common number of words in Prelutsky's prepositional phrases. (*Prelutsky has nine prepositional phrases with three words.*)

• Some prepositions can be used alone without a noun or noun phrase following them. Find two prepositions in Prelutsky's poem that can be used alone in a sentence. (Up *and* in *can be used alone in a sentence: for example,* he climbed up *or* he went in. *When prepositions are used alone, they function as adverbs.*)

• *On my stomach, in my hair, at my pillow,* and *on my head* are all prepositional phrases. Create an original definition for a prepositional phrase that compares a prepositional phrase to something else. (*Possible answers: a prepositional phrase is like a compass because it points out where something is, or a prepositional phrase is like a map because it locates things.*)

- List three situations in which you might use a lot of prepositional phrases to explain something. (*Possible answers: giving directions for traveling to a place, for cooking something, or for making a craft item.*)

Grammar Reinforcement Activities

At this point students have encountered prepositions through both reading and writing poetry, yet some students may need additional support. Use these activities to reinforce the basic concept and to provide an opportunity to discuss confusing features students may encounter. Consider which of these mini-lessons suits the ability level of your particular students and the amount of class time that you have available.

Visual:
Prepositions create a relationship between a noun and another word in the sentence. Students can make their own drawings with prepositional phrases. On $8\frac{1}{2}$- by 14-inch sheets of paper, have students draw their bedroom dream scene, with the bed located in the center of the picture. Students can include other rooms or an outdoor setting if they wish. Ask them to draw in at least five objects, such as doors, windows, and furniture, or rocks and plants if it's outdoors. Give students three to four identical small stickers to represent the animals or objects that they are dreaming about. (Reward stickers that are created for chore charts are very small and inexpensive and come in many different designs.) Have students place these stickers on their scenes. Using the list of prepositions given out earlier, have students write a prepositional phrase as a caption for each of the stickers.

Physical:
Have students play prepositional phrase hide-and-seek. Have a few students draw their poem animals or objects (or place stickers) on five sticky notes. Have one student close his or her eyes while the others hide the stickers. Have one student at a time, using his or her preposition word list, say a prepositional phrase clue, such as by the clock, near the door, behind the cabinet. Take turns hiding the stickers and giving prepositional phrase directions.

Grammar Extension Activity

An additional concept about prepositions can be introduced to students who want to learn more, or this activity can be used for an extra-credit assignment.

Object of the preposition:
Learning about phrases can help students to embed more details in their sentences. A prepositional phrase is made up of two or more words: the preposition and the noun or pronoun that is its object. Have students label the prepositions and underline the objects in all of the prepositional phrases in the source poem.

of <u>chickens</u>	up their <u>feathers</u>	in my <u>ears</u>
on my <u>stomach</u>	about my <u>bed</u>	on <u>top</u>
in my <u>hair</u>	on the <u>chairs</u> and <u>tables</u>	of <u>me</u>
at my <u>pillow</u>	on the <u>chandeliers</u>	
on my <u>head</u>	in the <u>corners</u>	

Explain that descriptive words, such as *my*, are often included in prepositional phrases. Have students add other adjectives to the prepositional phrase *in my hair*, such as *long*, *curly*, or *tangled*. Students can be challenged to make their prepositional phrases longer in their first stanza by adding a descriptive word before the noun.

Topic Variations

You can change the assignment to include objects as well as animals. Students can compose a "Dream" poem about

• shoes.

• ravioli.

• rainbows.

• homework.

• dirty dishes.

Writing About Literature

Students can compose a "Dream" poem about the values that are impor-tant to a literary character:

• for the classic fable, King Midas can dream about gold.

• for Sharon Creech's *Walk Two Moons*, Salamanca can dream about her mother.

Creech, S. (1994). *Walk two moons.* New York: HarperCollins.

Stewig, J. W. (1999). *King Midas: A golden tale.* New York: Holiday House.

Cloud and Sky

by Karla Kuskin

Cloud and sky.	1
Wet and dry.	2
Wind and weather.	3
Ice and cream.	4
Sleep and dream.	5
Some words seem	6
to go together.	7
Soft and skin.	8
Nose and chin.	9
Some words fit right in	10
together.	11

Pair Poems

¤ ¤ ¤ ¤ ¤ ¤ **Instructional Objective:** ¤ ¤ ¤ ¤ ¤ ¤ ¤

Students will write a "Pair" poem that contains six conjunctions.

Source Poem: "Cloud and Sky" by Karla Kuskin (reproducible page 59)

Introductory Activity

Distribute copies of "Cloud and Sky" by Karla Kuskin to the class. Have the class read the poem aloud in a way that emphasizes the connection between the paired words in each line. Divide the class in half, assigning the left side of the room to read the first word in the word pairs, and the right side to read the second word in the pairs. For example, the left side reads *cloud* and the right side reads *sky*. You serve as the connecting voice, reading the word *and* and all of the lines without *and* (6, 7, 10, and 11). For the second reading, have each side of the room quickly stand up when they read their word and then sit down when they are done. Have students read the word *together* in unison.

Modeling Activity

Imitate the model poem using new items. Begin by having students brainstorm a word bank of pairs of things that "go together." Record their ideas in two columns on the overhead, board, or chart paper. When the class runs out of ideas, look back at Kuskin's poem for ideas of categories such as nature, sensory words, weather, conditions, food, and daily actions. Have each student select a favorite pair from the class list and write a line in the format _____ *and* _____ on an index card or sticky note.

Have students work independently or with a small group to create two lines that rhyme. If students are having trouble, have a few volunteers share their rhyming lines with the class to clarify and reinforce the task. You might ask your strong auditory and musical learners to help their peers come up with rhymes.

Since rhyme lends itself to rhythm and music, you may want to have your students perform the class poem. Invite small groups of students to create music for the same class poem. Using impromptu percussion instruments like pencil cases and containers filled with paper clips or beans, have students perform the poem as a rap, a lullaby, a cowboy ballad, a jump-rope chant, a reggae tune, or a rock hit. Students can use the line *Some words seem to go together* or *Some words fit right in together* as a chorus. These performance poems can be videotaped and shared at a senior center.

Grammar Mini-Lesson

Three ways to define this concept are listed below. Consider which explanation will help your particular group of students understand the concept.

Question:
A coordinating conjunction joins equal elements—words, phrases, clauses, or sentences. We can locate conjunctions by asking the question *Which word joins, connects, compares, or contrasts two or more items?*

Meaning:
Coordinating conjunctions join things together. Conjunctions help to organize sentences, smoothly moving the reader along from one topic to another. Conjunctions can connect many different types of things, but the items must be of equal types in order to keep the meaning clear (*apples, bananas,* and *pears*—three nouns; *happy but uncertain*—two adjectives; *neither running nor skipping*—two gerunds). This is called *parallel structure* (see the Grammar Extension activity on page 65).

There are only seven coordinating conjunctions: *and, but, or, nor, for, yet, so.* These conjunctions all join things, but they have different meanings, establishing specific relationships among the items. The different meanings of the last four coordinating conjunctions may be challenging for students to grasp. *Nor* means "not this one either," *for* means "since" or "because," *yet* means "still" or "although," and *so* means "in order that."

Function:
A coordinating conjunction makes the sentence elements that it joins compound. Thus, the sentence may have two or more subjects, verbs, objects, descriptors, or clauses that function in the same way. For example, if *and* is used to join two or more subjects, all of the subjects do the same action (*Kerry and Jered will paint the fence*), but if *or* is used in the same case, only one of those subjects does the action (*Either Kerry or Jered will paint the fence*); in either case all of the subjects function as equals, and

> **TIP**
>
> Beginning writers can join words with coordinating conjunctions, while intermediate writers can join phrases and sentences in parallel constructions.

each pair becomes a *compound subject*. Conjunctions can be used to create compound predicates (*Kerry painted and cleaned up*) as well as compound sentences (*The robber offered a treat, but Rascal wouldn't stop barking*). Conjunctions can be used as a tool for condensing more information into one sentence, thus reducing the need to repeat words and create more sentences.

Have students examine the conjunctions in the source poem. Guide students to see that the one conjunction Kuskin uses is the most common coordinating conjunction, *and*. Then have them look at a piece of their own writing and tally up the coordinating conjunctions they've used. Have them look for places where they might add a conjunction to join two ideas and save space. Let students discuss with partners and share examples with the class.

Prewriting for an Individual Pattern Poem

Have students compose their own "Pair" poem. Ask them to jot down as many ideas as they can for pairs of words associated with sports, holidays, foods, music, fashions, places, famous people, pets, books, and movies.

Writing the Poem

Have students draft their own poems, imitating the repeating line structure of the original model. Remind them that each line must contain two words joined by the word *and*. Draw the frame below for students to use as a guide.

Pairs

_____ and _____. (Word)　　　(word)	1
_____ and _____. (Word)　　　(word)	2
_____ and _____. (Word)　　　(word)	3
_____ and _____. (Word)　　　(word)	4

Some words seem 　　　　　　　　　　5
to go together. 　　　　　　　　　　　6

_____ and _____. (Word)　　　(word)	7
_____ and _____. (Word)　　　(word)	8

Some words fit right in 　　　　　　　9
together. 　　　　　　　　　　　　　10

Publishing Activity

Students can publish their "Pair" poem on a woven magic card, following these directions:

1. Place a piece of $8\frac{1}{2}$- by 11-inch white paper horizontally in front of you, and fold the paper in half, side to side.

2. Fold each half back toward the center fold. Be sure to crease your folds repeatedly so that they will move smoothly. You will have four panels.

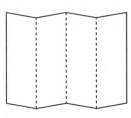

cut lines

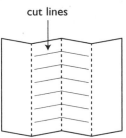

3. On the center fold, mark off six horizontal lines, forming seven spaces of about $1\frac{1}{4}$ inches each. Carefully, cut along each line to (but not through) the outside folds, so that when you open the paper, the two center panels have seven horizontal slits and the outer panels have none.

4. Cut two $8\frac{1}{2}$ by 2-inch strips of paper out of a colored sheet of construction paper.

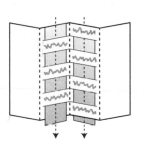

5. Weave the first strip in and out of panel two. Weave the second strip in the opposite way in and out of panel three.

6. Writing only on the white spaces, copy each of the seven lines of your poem onto the center two panels, alternating from panel two to panel three, leaving the contrasting colored spaces blank. (Note: Students will have to write small.)

7. With the paper sitting like a W (not an M), push the sides inward and then grab the two top white paper sections in the center and pull them apart, magically forming a new two-column set of strips, with the folded paper now looking like a V. Write the words from the last two lines, "Some words fit right in together," on the background paper, alternating sides, one word per space. Again, leave the contrasting colored spaces blank. One space will be left over for the author's name.

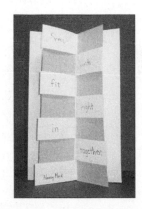

8. Pull the uncut panels outward from underneath to start the poem over. Write the title lengthwise on the first panel and conjuctions lengthwise on the fourth panel.

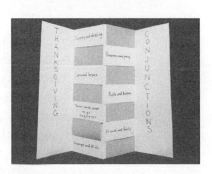

Teaching students how to make the magic card is easy once you've made a sample of the paper manipulative—use your sample to demonstrate. You might also teach this project first to one student or small group who needs extra support with sequencing and following directions. Let them practice and master the steps, and then teach it to the rest of the class.

Metacognitive Moment

Select some of the thought teasers below that are appropriate for your students. Have students discuss their ideas in small groups and then share their responses with the whole class for further wondering and discussion.

- Conjunctions can join two items or more in a series. Add an element to each of the pairs in Kuskin's poem, using only one *and*. (*Possible answers: cloud, sky, and breeze; wet, dry, and humid; wind, weather, and temperature; ice, cream, and cone; sleep, dream, and rest; soft, skin, and warm; nose, chin, and eyes.*)

- The coordinating conjunctions besides *and* are *but, or, nor, yet, so,* and *for*. Write pairs of words or sentences for each of the other conjunctions. (*Possible answers: tired but happy, friend or foe, neither happy nor sad, friendly yet cautious. So and for work best joining two sentences: She wanted to see time fly, so she threw the clock out the window. He practiced daily, for he wanted to make the team.*)

- *And, but, or, nor, yet, so,* and *for* are all conjunctions. Create an original definition that compares a prepositional phrase to something else. (*Answers might include: a conjunction is like a paper clip because it joins ideas together, or a conjunction is like a bridge between two roads.*)

- A chore rarely consists of just one action. Usually a chore involves several smaller tasks all related to one another. Write a sentence that lists four or more tasks you must do to complete a chore. Be sure that the items in your list are worded in a parallel way. (*A possible answer: I gather up all the wastebaskets, separate the cans, dump the trash into the big trash can, put the lid on the can, and haul it out to the curb.*)

Grammar Reinforcement Activities

At this point students have encountered conjunctions through reading and writing poetry, yet some students may need additional support. Use these activities to reinforce the basic concept and to provide an opportunity to discuss confusing features students may encounter. Consider which of these activities suits the ability level of your students and the amount of class time you have available.

Analogy:
Since conjunctions are the links that join parts together in a sentence, teachers need an analogy that can serve as a good visual model. In the past, teachers have used pictures of train couplers to represent conjunctions, but today's students are less familiar with trains. A more common substance used for joining a myriad of things together is duct tape. To demonstrate that conjunctions are like duct tape because they can join two words, write *word* on two filing cards and place the cards about 5 inches apart on a large piece of cardboard, and tape them to the

board with a single strip of duct tape that runs across the bottom of both cards. On the tape between the cards, write the word *conjunction* with permanent black marker. You can make the same model for other compound elements, "joining" pairs of cards with *phrases*, *clauses*, or *sentences* written on two cards.

Visual:
Another way to show that conjunctions connect or join things in a sentence is to use a pocket chart in which words can be moved around on cards. An inexpensive way to make word pockets is with envelopes and strip magnets. Take an average-sized envelope of about $6\frac{1}{2}$ inches or smaller and glue the flap inside for added strength. Using adhesive magnets by the roll or adhesive magnets for business cards (even half of one will work),

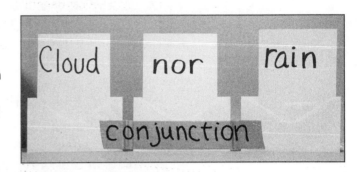

attach a magnet to the front of the envelope. Place the pocket envelope against the chalkboard or a metal cabinet with the back of the envelope outward to hold the filing cards. You will need three pockets for each line of paired words (*wind and rain*). Write one word onto the top half of each index card so that when it is placed in the envelope, the word will show. Be sure that the words being joined and the conjunction each have their own pocket. You can use duct tape to join the pockets front and back to make the analogy described above.

Grammar Extension Activity

An additional concept about conjunctions can be introduced to students who want to learn more, or this activity can be used for an extra-credit assignment.

Parallel Elements:
Conjunctions can join words, phrases, clauses, and sentences. Readers prefer balance in sentences so that the elements that are joined by a coordinating conjunction are all equal in type. For example, *plan a menu* and *house cleaning* are similar elements but not parallel. You can make these elements parallel by starting them with the same type of word: *menu planning* and *house cleaning* begin with a noun; *planning a menu* and *cleaning the house* begin with a gerund.

Challenge students to write a "Pair" poem that includes a coordinating pair of items in each line and that expands by two or more words with each successive line. Students can make the lines of their poems "grow" by joining words, phrases, clauses, and then sentences. Give them these tips: 1) Each line should have two parallel elements joined by the conjunction *and*; 2) Parallel sentence elements do not always have to have the same number of words, but they do need to be the same type of grammatical construction.

Thanksgiving

Family and friends.
Menu planning and house cleaning.
Finding the roaster and borrowing extra chairs.
Buying bags of groceries and spending hours cooking food.
Grandma brings the best pies, and children help set the table.
After all the food is prepared, and everything is carried to the table,
We give thanks for our bountiful blessings, and everyone fills a plate with
   delicious food.

Topic Variations

You can change the assignment to have students interview another person about his or her favorites. Students could write a "Pair" poem for

- a family member.
- a classmate.
- a younger student from another class.
- a media star.
- an animal.

Writing About Literature

Students can compose a "Pair" poem, comparing the traits of two literary characters

- in the classic fable, the Hare and the Tortoise represent opposites in behavior and philosophy.

- in Rodman Philbrick's *Freak the Mighty*, Kevin and Max become friends and have different abilities.

Philbrick, R. (1993). *Freak the Mighty*. New York: Blue Sky Press.

Ward, H. (1999). *Hare and the Tortoise*. Brookfield, CT: Millbrook Press.

Boa Constrictor

by Shel Silverstein

Oh, I'm being eaten	1
By a boa constrictor,	2
A boa constrictor,	3
A boa constrictor,	4
I'm being eaten by a boa constrictor,	5
And I don't like it—one bit.	6
Well, what do you know?	7
It's nibblin' my toe.	8
Oh, gee,	9
It's up to my knee.	10
Oh my,	11
It's up to my thigh.	12
Oh, fiddle,	13
It's up to my middle.	14
Oh, heck,	15
It's up to my neck.	16
Oh, dread,	17
It's up mmmmmmmmmmfffffffff. . .	18

Extraordinary Experience Poems

> ⌑ ⌑ ⌑ ⌑ ⌑ ⌑ **Instructional Objective:** ⌑ ⌑ ⌑ ⌑ ⌑ ⌑ ⌑
>
> Students write an "Extraordinary Experience" poem that contains 12 interjections.
>
> Source Poem: "Boa Constrictor" by Shel Silverstein (reproducible page 67)

Introductory Activity

Distribute copies of "Boa Constrictor" by Shel Silverstein to the class. In call-and-response fashion have the class read the even-numbered lines while you read the odd-numbered lines, which are the interjection lines. This poem employs deadpan humor—note that Silverstein avoids using exclamation marks. You may want to read the interjections in an ironic manner, as if you are bored. For the second reading, have students stand to read their lines and add simple gestures to some of their lines. For example, they can touch their toes, then their knees, and so on, to indicate the progress of the boa constrictor.

Modeling Activity

Imitate the model poem using a new extraordinary experience. Begin by having students select an experience, such as parachuting from a plane, sinking into quicksand, or getting lost in a cave. Model writing the opening lines on the overhead, board, or chart paper, including information about what causes the experience or where the experience occurs. It may be easiest to compose the fifth line of the poem first (*I'm* + extraordinary experience / *and I don't like it—one bit*) and then break this line apart to form lines one through four.

Next, have students brainstorm a list of interjections that the narrator in the new poem might say, including the ones from the model poem: *oh, my, gee, fiddle, heck, dread, shoot, darn, rats, oops, no, eek, wow, yikes, ack, ugh,* boo, *sniff*, *sigh*, *aye*, *ouch*, and so forth. Students each select one of the inter-jections and write two paired lines on an index card or sticky note: one interjection line and one extraordinary experience line. Make sure students see that the pattern for the first line is two paired interjections, *oh* and another choice (*my*, *heck*, and so on). If necessary, rewrite the lines together, to ensure that students can imitate the pattern.

Ask students to share their lines. Record them on the board and then have the class determine the sequence in which they should be placed, as well as a funny ending.

This poem can be read dramatically and may be fun for students to perform as Readers Theater for another class or individually for a friend with a good sense of humor. Brainstorm what type of movement and vocal treatment would best suit the extraordinary experience. For instance, if the poem is about falling, students could start out standing and gradually lower themselves to the floor as they say their lines. Students could draw out the last word in a fading voice to make it sound as if they were falling.

> **Skydiving**
>
> Oh, I'm falling
> Out of
> A plane,
> A plane,
> I'm falling out of a plane,
> And I don't like it—one bit.
> Well, what do you know?
> I am falling down.
> Oh, gee,
> Look at me.
> Oh my,
> I can't fly!
> Oh, pain,
> This sport is insane.
> Oh my,
> I'll surely die!
> Oh, shoot,
> No parachute!

TIP

Since the point of the modeling activity is to imitate the grammar element rather than the sound element, it is not necessary that the lines of the class poem rhyme. Students can attempt rhyme later for the revision activity.

Grammar Mini-Lesson

Three ways to define this concept are listed below. Consider which explanation will help your particular group of students understand the concept.

Question:

An interjection is an interrupting word or words that express emotion. We can locate interjections by asking the question *Which word expresses emotion and is added on to the sentence?*

Meaning:

An interjection is an emotional expression that is often informal and sounds like oral speech even when it's not part of dialogue. Interjections may be slang words, nonsense words, or just a sound or vocalization like *ouch* or *oops*. An interjection may be an idiom or idiolect expression of an expletive. For example, *Good golly, Miss Molly* is an idiom that is used by an older age group, and *whoopsie, doopsie, doodle* is an idiolect expression created by one person. Beginning writers may overload their writing with interjections, while novelists use them only in appropriate situations, such as in an emotion-filled line of dialogue.

Function:

Interjections are independent words added on to a sentence, most commonly at the beginning, but they can be added at the end or elsewhere in a sentence. Since interjections have no direct function or grammatical relationship with the other words in the sentence, some linguists do not believe that interjections are important enough to be called a part of speech that is equal to nouns and verbs. One way to test a word to see if it is an interjection is to see if it can be dropped out of the sentence. If removing it from the sentence also takes away some of the emotional impact of the sentence, then that's an even stronger case for labeling it an interjection.

Have students examine the interjections in the source poem (*well, oh, gee, my, fiddle, heck,* and *dread*) and then flag with sticky notes other examples of interjections used in literature they are reading. Have them share their examples and let the class determine whether the example features an interjection. Ask them whether they think they would be more likely to find interjections in fiction or nonfiction writing. (*Most likely, you'd find interjections in fiction, where there's an emotional context for events and the author includes characters' spoken words; however, you may find interjections in some nonfiction forms, such as letters to the editor or in quotations used in news stories.*)

Prewriting for an Individual Pattern Poem

Have students compose their own "Extraordinary Experience" poems for an unfortunate event. As a class, brainstorm awful situations, such as losing money, breaking something valuable, failing a class, and being in the middle of a storm.

Have each student select an extraordinary experience about which he or she wants to write. Tell students to jot down as many ideas as they can for the events of their chosen experience, such as how it began, what happened next, bad results, negative feelings, terrible consequences, and worst fears.

Writing the Poem

Have students draft their own poems, imitating the paired line structure of the original model, with one line containing interjections and the other line describing the experience. Draw the frame below for students to use as a guide.

_____
(Extraordinary Experience)

Oh, I'm _____
      (-*ing* action word)

_____
(how/from where)
A/an _____,
     (source)
A/an _____,
     (source)
I'm _____ _____, _____
   (-*ing* action word) (how/from where) (source)
And I don't like it—one bit.
Well, what do you know?
I'm _____ _____.
   (-*ing* action word) (from where)
Oh, _____,
    (interjection)
I'm _____.
 (extraordinary experience)
Oh, _____,
    (interjection)
I'm _____.
 (extraordinary experience)
Oh, _____,
    (interjection)
I'm _____.
 (extraordinary experience)
Oh, _____,
    (interjection)
I'm _____.
 (extraordinary experience)
Oh, _____,
    (interjection)
I'm _____.
 (extraordinary concluding experience)

TIP

Remember that the first four lines of the poem are simply the fifth line of the poem split up into four parts. In fact, it may be easiest to write the fifth line first and then just break it into the four opening lines of the poem.

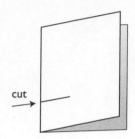

Publishing Activity

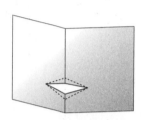

Students can publish their "Extraordinary Experience" poem in a pop-up mouth card by following these directions:

1. Place a piece of $8\frac{1}{2}$-inch white paper horizontally in front of you and fold the paper in half, side to side.

2. Cut a 1-inch slit perpendicular to the fold to create the mouth. Make the cut near the bottom of the fold to allow for more room for the face.

3. Keeping the card closed, fold the paper back from the slit to form two triangle flaps. Crease the two folds repeatedly, bending them forward and backward, to be sure that they will move smoothly. Unfold the triangle flaps and open the card. Push the paper in (toward the inside of the card) from the fold on both the top and the bottom of the slit. Crease well. This creates an open diamond on the back of the card and pop-up triangle-pairs on the inside.

4. Fold another sheet of paper in half, side to side, and slide it over the outside of the sheet with the pop-up mouth. Match up the edges and glue the sheets together, dabbing the glue lightly in all four corners.

5. Open the card to reveal the moving mouth. Draw a face around the mouth to represent the surprised narrator.

6. Write the poem on the front of the card or on the left side of the face. Write a list of all of the interjection words used in the poem on the right side of the mouth.

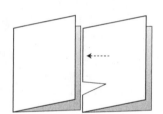

Invite the art teacher or building support staff to view students' pop-up mouth cards.

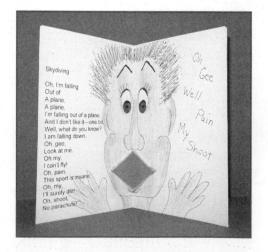

Metacognitive Moment

Select some of the thought teasers below that are appropriate for your students. Have students discuss their ideas in small groups and then share their responses with the whole class for further wondering and discussion.

- List the two interjections that Silverstein uses that are onomatopoeic or sound words. (*Oh* and *gee* *are onomatopoeic words.*) List five other onomatopoeic words that could be used as interjections. (*Possible answers: oops, eek, wow, yikes, ack, ugh, boo, sniff, sigh, aye, and ouch.*)

- *Well, oh, gee, my, fiddle, heck,* and *dread* are all interjections. Create an original definition that compares an interjection to something else. (*Possible answers: an interjection is like a cheer at a basketball game because it expresses emotion and interrupts the action, or an interjection is like a commercial on TV because it interrupts the show and sometimes it tries to sell things by appealing to emotions.*)

- Name the interjection in the poem that can refer to a musical instrument or the playing of an instrument. Tell what this interjection means and whether it is an idiom that is used informally by a particular group of people. (*Fiddle refers to a violin or another stringed instrument. It may also act as a verb, as in "to fiddle around," meaning to waste time. In this poem, however, it acts as an interjection that expresses only a little concern, like* gee *and* heck.)

- Make a list of ten positive circumstances that would cause a person to yell out happy interjections. (*Possible answers: winning the lottery, finding money, earning a good grade, getting a phone call from someone important, receiving a present.*)

Grammar Reinforcement Activities

At this point students have encountered interjections through reading and writing poetry, yet some students may need additional support. Use these activities to reinforce the basic concept and to provide an opportunity to discuss confusing features students may encounter. Consider which of these activities suits the ability level of your students and the amount of class time you have available.

Analogy:
Interjections are added to a sentence and express emotion, much like the popular emoticons used for e-mail and instant messaging. For example:

> Hope to see you later, ☺.

Interjections can represent the same emotion as the emoticons by using a word or phrase. Have students print out five or more emoticons and then write a corresponding interjection to represent that emoticon in words. In addition, students can draw emoticons next to the interjections that they add to the dialogue in the next activity to cue the actors.

Physical:

Interjections can totally change the meaning of a sentence. Have a pair of students read the dialogue below without emotion. Then invite the class to add an interjection to each line, expressing different emotions, such as fear, boredom, humor, jealousy, or sadness. Have volunteers act out the rewritten sentences with different interjections and emotions.

> **A Dialogue About a Snake**
> SPEAKER ONE: I got a snake for my birthday.
> SPEAKER TWO: A snake?
> SPEAKER ONE: A big snake.
> SPEAKER TWO: Are you kidding me?
> SPEAKER ONE: Take a look at it.
> SPEAKER TWO: I am going home.
> SPEAKER ONE: Don't you like my snake?
> SPEAKER TWO: I have to go.

Grammar Extension Activity

Introduce this additional concept about interjections to students who want to learn more, or use this activity as an extra-credit assignment.

Punctuation:

Since an interjection is an independent addition to a sentence, it is normally separated from the rest of a sentence with various forms of punctuation. These example sentences show how the same interjection can be set off different ways:

> Oops, Cinderella lost her shoe.
> When she ran away, Cinderella lost her shoe—oops.
> The accidental loss of her shoe (oops) was just a trick to get the Prince's attention.

However, if the interjection expresses strong emotion, it receives an exclamation mark right after it:

> Hurray! At last the Prince had found Cinderella.

Challenge students to determine whether each of the interjections in their "Extraordinary Experience" poems should have a comma or an exclamation point. In proofreading pairs, have students explain to their partners why they chose the punctuation marks that they did. Remind them that Silverstein chose to use commas rather than exclamation marks, making his poem humorous by having the narrator underreact to the snake.

Topic Variations

You can change the assignment to be an extraordinary experience that is positive or humorous. Students can write an "Extraordinary Experience" poem about

* winning a contest.
* finding a lost pet.
* a favorite team winning the playoffs.
* getting a good grade on a test.
* seeing a rainbow.

Writing About Literature

Have students compose an "Extraordinary Experience" poem about the complications that a literary character experiences:

* for nursery rhymes "Jack Horner," "Little Miss Muffet," and "Little Bo Peep," the characters have different surprises to report.
* for Louis Sachar's *Holes*, Stanley's digging produces interesting results.

Lobel, A. (1991). *The Random House Book of Mother Goose.* New York: Random House.

Sachar, L. (1998). *Holes.* New York: Farrar, Straus and Giroux.

Supporting Language Learning Beyond the Grammar Lessons in This Book

We teachers are interested not only in what works, but also in why it works. In this chapter, you'll find some of the broader theories about language learning that have helped me to develop the grammar lessons in this book—and that may help you to develop new methods for language arts instruction in your own classroom. I address four guiding questions about language instruction and how research supports nontraditional approaches. For each question, I mention some practical applications and cite scholars whose work may inspire you and inform your practice. References are included on page 81.

How can we build on students' natural language learning?

No matter how many times I read what literacy expert Frank Smith has to say about how children learn language, I am amazed by how much children learn before they come to school. In *Understanding Reading* (1994), Smith says that children "invent grammar," meaning that each child "discovers" the grammar system through trial and error. Smith describes the process of learning to speak as hypothesis testing, feedback evaluation, and theory construction; errors are an important part of the process of learning complex language rules.

Children's speech is full of examples of grammar "mistakes" that are evidence of their growing understanding of language. For example, linguist Constance Weaver (1996) explains how errors like *goed* instead of *went* reveal that a child is intuitively inventing the past-tense rule for regular verbs ending in *-ed*. Children become increasingly facile with language as they practice speaking and later, writing. Brian Cambourne's work with early literacy emphasizes that the child's first attempts are global approximations, but with later performances, the child's language eventually becomes more detailed and exact (1998). The challenge becomes how to respect errors as a part of developmental growth rather than condemn them as signs of total ignorance.

The key, I believe, is to tap students' intuitive knowledge about grammar and let them wonder about language through discussion with their peers and teacher. In the grammar lessons I've included here, I use the Metacognitive Moment activities to help students consciously theorize about how language works (*Is the pattern the same in each line of the poem?*). A great way to use these prompts is to have a weekly 15-minute "language lab" session in which students analyze a language pattern or convention within real texts, using a discovery process of asking and then answering their own questions. Of course, there are many ways to set up this language lab session—from small group work, to individual response notebooks that are shared, to partner discussions that feed into whole-class discussions, The idea is to create an atmosphere of wondering in your classroom that lets students actively make sense of how language works.

How can we help students take even greater control of their language learning?

When I first started teaching, I had been taught to discourage any social interaction among my students to avoid "distractions" from teaching. After reading the theories of cognitive psychologist, Lev Vygotsky (1986), I began to understand the critical importance of social interaction to all learning. Educational scholars now use Vygotsky's notion of the zone of proximal development (1975) to explain how a student's intelligence can be increased with slight assistance from a teacher or another student. The mentor provides a supportive scaffold to guide the student's performance with the least intervention possible. This scaffolding approach requires a lot of social dialogue to question, extend students' ideas further, and get feedback from learners, so the mentor can help them progress.

Other Vygotskian concepts are equally useful for educators. Vygotsky's work on inner speech (1986) maps out how social talk eventually becomes internalized as thought processes. In the same way we introduce students to math concepts with models and concrete manipulatives, we must also introduce language concepts through purposeful talk before we can expect students to internalize grammar terms. Consider the amount of time you allow students to discuss new language concepts before you ask them to apply the concept in their writing. Is it enough? Have you allowed time for them to figure out how they already use it or how it might help them communicate? (See the metacognitive discussion on page 77.)

MAKING INSTRUCTION A LEARNING PROCESS FOR YOU, THE TEACHER

When you finally get a strategy to work after trying it repeatedly and changing this or that, ask yourself, what made the method work? Think about your process metacognitively. If you can articulate why a particular strategy worked, then you can likely invent other strategies based on what you've discovered.

One of Vygotsky's most important areas of study was high-level thought processes. He believed that these thought processes enable human beings to adapt to the environment by increasing their own inner self-regulation or self-control. When we apply this notion to education, our aim is to teach students how to think so that they can control themselves and make the most of their learning experiences. Regrettably, teachers are pressured to monitor students' behavior, marking every error students make while learning. However, controlling students is not the same as teaching them self-control.

We must find ways to help students manage their own writing rather than merely correcting workbook sentences or waiting for the teacher to correct their writing for them. When we support students with good models, guided instruction, choice, and a joyful purpose for communicating, students take responsibility for their writing. They become invested in the product and the real audience with whom it will be shared. My students always request more time and help with proofreading when they care about their writing. This is why the grammar lessons in this book emphasize writing meaningful poetry that is artistically published so that students will be proud to celebrate their writing with others. Consider the different audiences to whom students might present their written work and the types of publication formats that will build excitement and enthusiasm for their writing. Can you create new audiences within the school or bring in families and other community members who may find specific projects interesting? What successful publishing formats do your colleagues use?

TIP

Motivation, choice, and purpose are important ingredients for students' development as self-sufficient writers.

How can language instruction become more compatible with brain research?

The brain seems to be hardwired to perceive patterns. Research with newborn infants has demonstrated that they prefer patterns that look like faces. Human beings find and create patterns everywhere. Math is taught as numerical patterns. Linguists diagram sentences into schematic trees that look amazingly similar to chemical or mathematical formulas. Artists and musicians create repeated patterns that appeal to our aesthetic sensibility. Our brains recognize patterns after we have gathered enough data from real-life experience. All these patterns—facial, numerical, linguistic, chemical, artistic, musical—help us to make sense of the world. In fact, new information only makes sense to us when we can associate it with a pattern that we already know. In other words, unless we can place the new information within an existing pattern, it just doesn't make sense to us and we reject or forget it.

Patterns are essential to learning. When we have no choice but to learn things that do not seem to make any sense to us or do not have an easily recognizable pattern, we associate or link the new learning into a familiar pattern. When we consciously create ways to remember new information by placing it within patterns that we will remember, we create mnemonic devices—medical students use rhymes and visual associations to remember anatomy, and chemical engineers make humorous sentences from the first letters of terms that they need to memorize. Similarly, when our students cannot make sense of particular spelling and grammar conventions, we can encourage them to use memory by association. For instance, students can use mnemonic devices for learning spelling and usage patterns, such as the reminder *principal* has *-pal* at the end because the principal is your pal.

My own breakthrough in teaching came about when I began to think of usage rules as a pattern of language use that society has sanctioned as "preferred." I have come to see that one type of grammar or one dialect is not inherently better than another; language conventions are just accepted habits that change over time. Moreover, what is accepted by the larger society as standard and what is considered substandard is undoubtedly a political choice that has racial, class, and gender implications, which I discuss with my students. As their teacher, I never, never devalue my students' home languages—this is particularly critical because research shows that students may equate a rejection of their home language with a feeling of discomfort and exclusion from school itself (Penrose, 2002). However, I also recognize that my students must learn preferred patterns of language in order to participate fully in the world in which we live. So I teach my students to discover language patterns and to work and play with those patterns, as they do when they imitate and make variations on a model poem. In this way, the patterns become familiar and students gain ownership of them through using them. My goal is for them to gain mastery of "academic" English in addition to their home language, so that they can use both languages effectively for their own purposes.

How can we make grammar instruction fit within the context of meaningful student writing?

If you are interested in learning about the history of language instruction, you will find a great resource in the work of Constance Weaver (1996), who does an excellent job summarizing, discussing, and analyzing several major studies about grammar instruction. Weaver reminds us that as long ago as 1936 the National Council of Teachers of English recommended that grammar no longer be taught separately from writing instruction. Moreover, Weaver explains a great deal about the possibilities for teaching grammar through writing. Of particular use are suggestions to teach grammar and usage in mini-lessons that reflect students' developmental needs as writers. For example, skills such as sentence manipulation need to be taught using both excellent models as well as students' own ideas and writing. In a related anthology volume (1998), Weaver includes many individual approaches to embedding grammar instruction in the writing process.

Using Weaver's and my own research, I have grouped current approaches to teaching grammar in the context of meaningful writing into three categories:

- teaching students to recognize grammar elements and sentence patterns through guided writing assignments,

- teaching advanced syntax patterns through sentence combining during revision, and

- teaching students to correct their own usage errors during editing and proofreading.

The lessons in this volume fit mainly into the first category although there are some editing activities that address usage issues. I recommend using all three of these approaches regularly, provided they are used in the context of real student writing.

A major problem you may encounter with published instructional materials is that these materials tend to isolate language study from students' writing. For example, the second approach, sentence combining, is an excellent way to get students to try out more sophisticated sentence structures; however, sentence combining activities generally take the form of workbook pages. Materials developed for the third approach, usage mini-lessons, are frequently published as daily writing drills. Using these materials gives teachers a concrete way to cover specific skills and prepare students for taking tests. However, it is an ineffective way to get students to apply what they've learned to their own writing. Error correction just doesn't transfer to improving student writing when it is practiced on phony example sentences.

As a profession, we are only just learning how to move away from workbook pages to find teachable moments during authentic writing practice. Consider ways you can weave direct instruction and thoughtful reflection about language into real and meaningful writing experiences for your students. Inside of every patterned poem, there is a grammar mini-lesson just waiting to be discovered.